THE BODMIN & WENFORD RAILWAY

• A PAST AND PRESENT COMPANION •

BODMIN AND WADEBRIDGE RAILWAY.

PASSENGER TRAINS,

October, 1871,

AND UNTIL FURTHER NOTICE.

MONDAY:	Wadebridge to Bodmin,	at 10. 0	A. M.
	Bodmin, to Wadebridge,	„ 4. 0	P. M.
WEDNESDAY:	Wadebridge to Bodmin,	„ 10. 0	A. M.
	Bodmin to Wadebridge,	„ 4. 0	P. M.
FRIDAY:	Wadebridge to Bodmin,	„ 10. 0	A. M.
	Bodmin to Wadebridge,	„ 4. 0	P. M.
SATURDAY:	Wadebridge to Bodmin,	„ 1. 0	P. M.
	Bodmin to Wadebridge,	„ 2.30	„
	Wadebridge to Bodmin,	„ 4.30	„
	Bodmin to Wadebridge,	„ 7. 0	„

H. KYD, Superintendent.

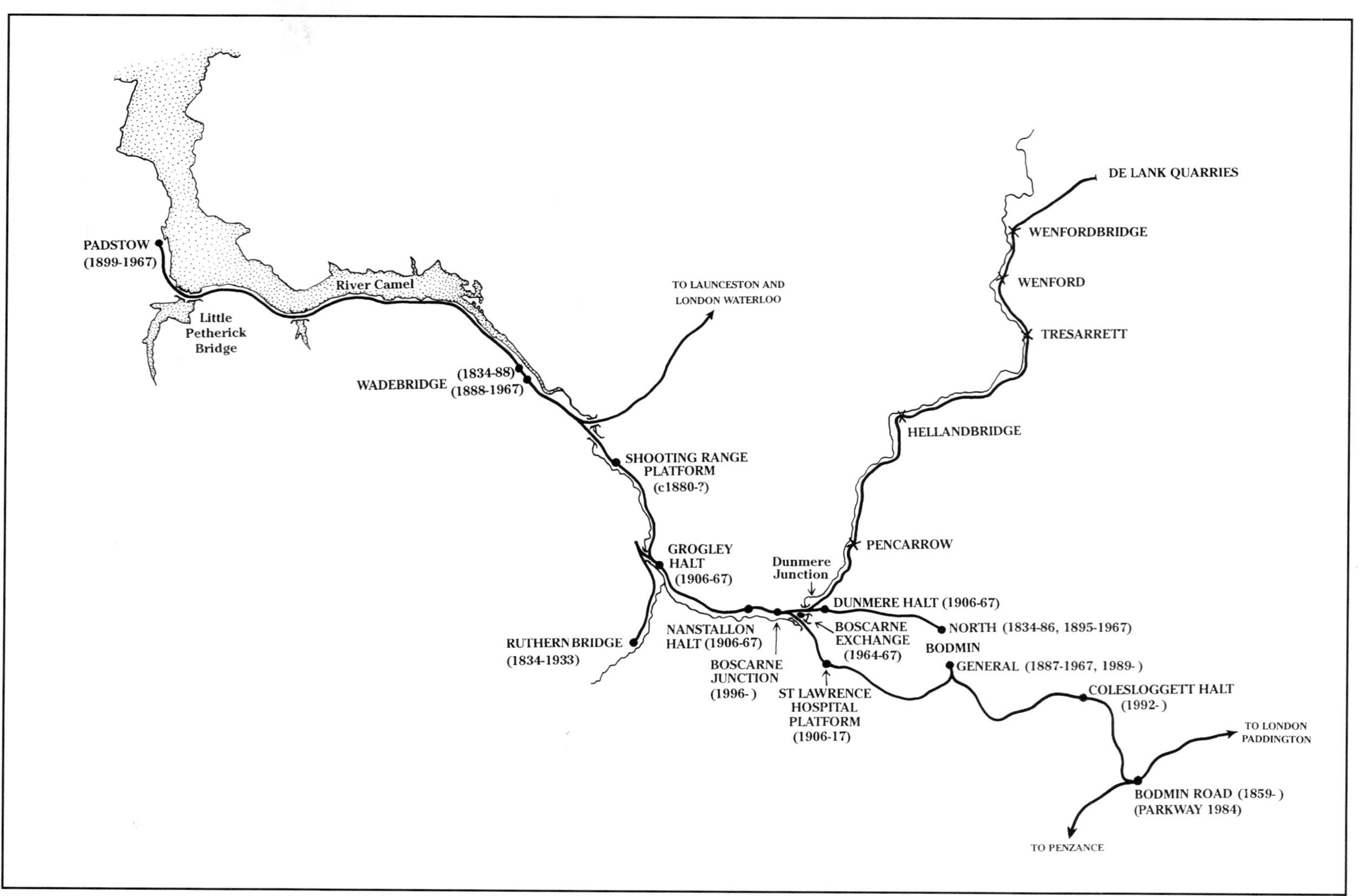

Map of the Bodmin & Wenford Railway and associated lines.

THE BODMIN & WENFORD RAILWAY

• A PAST AND PRESENT COMPANION •

A nostalgic trip along the whole route from Bodmin Road to Wadebridge and Padstow

John Stretton

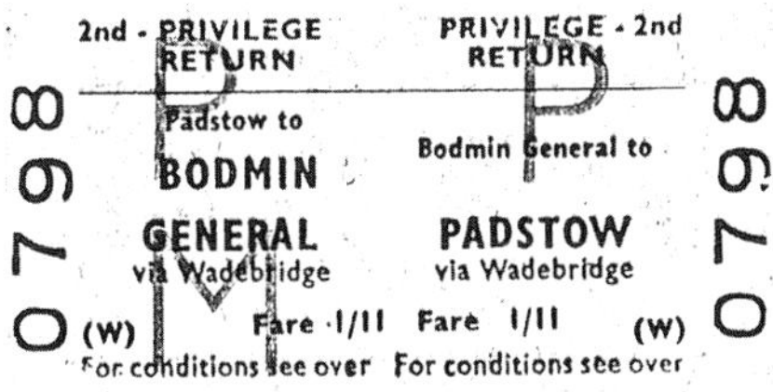

• RAILWAY HERITAGE •

from

The NOSTALGIA *Collection*

First published in April 1999

British Library Cataloguing in Publication Data

A catalogue record for this book is available from the British Library.

ISBN 1 85895 135 6

Past & Present Publishing Ltd
The Trundle
Ringstead Road
Great Addington
Kettering
Northants NN14 4BW

Tel/Fax: 01536 330588
email: sales@slinkp-p.demon.co.uk

Map drawn by Christina Siviter

All the 'present' photographs were taken by the author in either March or May 1998.

Printed and bound in Great Britain

Past and Present

A Past & Present book
from
The* NOSTALGIA *Collection

ACKNOWLEDGEMENTS

Before I began this book, I knew of the Bodmin & Wenford Railway and some of the historical attractions of the area, but I had not sampled them at first hand. Such has been the welcome, courtesy and co-operation of all concerned that I now feel very much at home when visiting the railway and a enjoy a warm sense of well-being whenever the area is thought of or mentioned. This is due in no small part to the very special help given by all involved, some of whom deserve a special mention.

First must come Maurice Dart. His welcome, knowledge, contacts, collection of relevant material and his company on my exploration of the routes between Bodmin and Wadebridge/Wenfordbridge were pleasant and invaluable. Without his knowledge of the Wenford/Wenfordbridge area, I would have been, almost literally, lost!

Peter Treloar has also been of immense help, both before and after the selection of the photographs; Roger Webster and Keith Searle of the B&W have accommodated this interloper at times of great pressure with courtesy and assistance; and all the photographers whose material is used herein have all, without exception, been ready with their help and co-operation. Thus I have ended by learning a lot and deriving very real pleasure from this project, and I hope that the reader will share at least some of this.

Thanks must also go to the publishers for their faith and support; and certainly not least to my long-suffering wife Judi, who has borne with great fortitude and patience the frustrations of piles of photographs, books and boxes littering the house. I hope everyone feels it has been worth it!

CONTENTS

BODMIN AND WADEBRIDGE RAILWAY.

PAY SHEET.

Fortnight ending June 13th 1867

WAY AND WORKS.

NAME.	TIME.	RATE PER WEEK.	AMOUNT. £.	s.	d.	TOTAL. £.	s.	d.
[illegible] Inch.	12 days	17/.	1	14	0			
W. Pendray	12 "	16/-	1	12	0			
Jos. Hicks	12 "	"	1	12	0			
J. Webber.	12	14/.	1	8	0			
J. Higman	11 "	"	1	5	8			
J. Sweet.	2 "	22/.	.	7	4			
J. Bunny	4 "	18/.	.	12	0			
W. Worden	4 "	14/.	.	9	4			
Jon. Lobb.	2 "	19/.	.	6	4			
J. Blake	4 "	14/.	.	9	4			
R. Menhinick.	8 "	25/.	1	13	4			
						11	9	4

Delightfully setting the scene for the start of our journey is this highly evocative view of what steam on our railways and holidays in the West Country were all about. On a wonderfully sunny 4 July 1959, 'Grange' Class 4-6-0s Nos 6832 *Brockton Grange* and 6825 *Llanvair Grange* double-head what looks to be a 13-coach 8.15am Perranporth-Paddington service away from Bodmin Road station. The gradient post to the right of the leading buffer beam indicates the immediate 1 in 85 climb, but the train has 5 miles of more or less straight climbing from here to Doublebois and the locos and crews will both be working hard.

Bodmin Road, 274 miles from Paddington by the 'direct' route, originally opened in broad gauge days on 27 June 1859, had its name changed to Bodmin Parkway in May 1984 and is now the interchange station for the preserved Bodmin & Wenford Railway. *Peter Gray*

INTRODUCTION

If the Bodmin & Wenford Railway was a cat, it would have already used several of its lives! The railways operating to the two destinations have 'diced with death' on a number of occasions, and it is through no small slice of luck that the present happy sight of the preservation movement in the area has been enjoyed by many thousands.

In at the birth of railways in this country, the Bodmin & Wadebridge Railway was one of a small coterie of operations that showed the way ahead and set the seal on the 'railway mania' that was to follow. It was the brainchild of Sir William Molesworth of Pencarrow, a local landowner and, later, member of Palmerston's Government. Just a handful of lines had been built when the B&W opened its first route, including the Stockton & Darlington, Liverpool & Manchester, Canterbury & Whitstable and Leicester & Swannington, the latter opening just two years earlier in 1832. Note that none had yet surfaced in London!

Authorised by an Act of Parliament in 1832, building started from Wadebridge, reaching Bodmin in July 1834 and Ruthern Bridge and Wenfordbridge two months later. At this distance in time it is difficult to appreciate the very real gamble that the railway was taking, being completely isolated from any other, and in a part of the country itself isolated by poor roads and/or long sea journeys from the great population centres.

The line's raison d'être was the transport of sea sand inland for use as an agricultural fertiliser – indeed, passenger services were almost non-existent for the first 30 years. There was some downwards mineral traffic, but financial pressures were already apparent by 1845 when the broad gauge Cornwall Railway made a bid for the B&W. A counter bid was made by the 'standard' gauge Cornwall & Devon Central Railway, but both were to fail, leaving the baton to be picked up (somewhat illegally for the first 40 years) by the London & South Western Railway in 1846. The B&W thus became part of the LSWR empire, but at the time a somewhat tenuous connection, as the LSWR tracks were still 200 miles away!

The B&W finally joined the rest of the railway map in 1888, ironically thanks to the LSWR's rival in the area, the Great Western Railway! On 27 May 1887 the link was completed from Bodmin Road (opened in 1859 on the broad gauge main line from London) to Bodmin (later 'General'), and 15 months later on to Boscarne Junction, where physical union was made with the route from Wenfordbridge. It was to be a further seven years before the LSWR finally extended its arm to Wadebridge from Okehampton and Launceston, over what became known as the North Cornwall route. Padstow was finally reached in March 1899.

There was a 'brief' hiatus in passenger services to Bodmin (North) between 1886 and 1895 while a new station was built. After that, other than the closure of the short 1½-mile branch to Ruthern Bridge in 1933, traffic settled into a pattern, largely uninterrupted by war except for the occasional use of the line from Bodmin Road to Wadebridge as a diversion to the GWR's main line to Exeter. In due course Dr Beeching turned his gaze toward the locality, and from 1 January 1963 all traffic in the area was transferred to the Western Region.

Initial moves towards dieselisation were not overly successful, and in 1964 through services from Bodmin North to Wadebridge were terminated, passengers being merely taken to a new exchange platform at Boscarne Junction, there to connect with the Bodmin General trains. October 1966 saw the closure of the North Cornwall route to Wadebridge after two years of trials with diesels, and January 1967 was the death knell for the Bodmin North experiment, and for passenger trains from Bodmin Road westwards and all services to Padstow. Freight struggled on to Wadebridge until 2 September 1978, when the section from Boscarne Junction was fully closed, leaving only the china clay freight services from

Wenfordbridge to the main line at Bodmin Road. This traffic succumbed in September 1983.

For around 70 years three Beattie 2-4-0 Well Tanks were the mainstay of freight haulage, a class originally built between 1862 and 1875 for London suburban services; the trio long outlived their sisters, the last of which had been withdrawn in 1898! In August 1962 they were displaced by three GWR '1366' Class locos, but these only lasted a year and the work was then turned over to diesels, firstly Class 03 shunters, then 08s.

This could have been the end of the story, especially as the track was removed between Boscarne Junction and Wenfordbridge, enabling North Cornwall District Council to open the whole of the route from Padstow as a footpath and cycle track, known as the Camel Trail. However, a small band of enthusiasts had other ideas.

The Bodmin Railway Preservation Society was formed in 1984 with a view to re-opening as much of the local railways as possible, and a year later shares were issued by the Bodmin & Wenford Railway plc. This was to enable the purchase of the section where track was still laid, from Bodmin Parkway (as Bodmin Road was by then known) to Boscarne Junction, including the station at Bodmin General. In 1989 a Light Railway Order was obtained and services began. A regular timetable between General and Parkway was instituted from the summer of 1990, and since then visitor turnover has grown substantially.

Over the years, as well as restoring its own locos and rolling-stock on site, the railway has arranged prestigious visits by others, such as *City of Truro* in 1992, 'Prairie' tank No 4561, No 1450 plus autocoach, and, perhaps most notably in 1998, No 6024 *King Edward I*. The first official visit to Cornwall by a 'King' Class locomotive, it not only brought thousands of extra visitors to the railway during its three-week stay, but perhaps more importantly also raised the profile of the railway locally. Since the visit, the B&W has won many new local converts to its restoration plans. From 1990 to 1992 the railway was also able to assist with commercial freight movements for Fitzgerald Lighting from Bodmin to the main line at Bodmin Parkway, repeated in 1998 thanks to the enlightened approach of English, Welsh & Scottish Railways (EWS) towards small-wagon-load traffic.

So, back from the brink once more, much attention is being given to the legal obstacles to the proposed reopening to Wenford. It is recognised that restoring the china clay traffic to rail would be both economically agreeable to English China Clay International Ltd and ecologically very desirable, by taking in excess of 8,300 lorry journeys annually from highly unsuitable, narrow country roads. Between 1994 and 1996 fortunes have seesawed, with permission to re-open being granted and reversed. A public enquiry at Bodmin in February 1996 ruled against the railway, but in November 1996 the Secretary of State once more overturned the decision, granting the LRO to the railway. The B&W, it seemed, breathed again, but still matters were not over!

Despite the trackbed of the Camel Trail not being officially a public right of way, a vocal minority, led by the Camel Trail Preservation Group, obtained another judicial review, when again the LRO was overturned! North Cornwall District Council, previously supporting the reinstatement, now turned against the project, compounding the difficulties. The B&W, however, is made of stern stuff and through 1997 and 1998 took advice and subsequent steps to try to regain its LRO. An Environmental Assessment was begun in the summer of 1998 and completed in the autumn, a prerequisite to any sanction for the reopening; the railway has accepted the principle of providing an alternative Trail wherever possible; ECCI Ltd is being asked for commitments regarding a switch to rail if available; and pressure has been applied to the Department of Transport and regional authorities to give the 'go-ahead' as soon as the above points have been satisfactorily concluded. With EWS sympathetic to the reinstatement of the china clay traffic, and the Government's avowed wish to see more freight by rail, it is to be hoped that the Secretary of State will be equally sympathetic to the cause and reinstate the LRO. The prospect of seeing china clay 'hoods' wending their way back to Wenford – and even the return of passengers to Wadebridge – fills all supporters of the Bodmin & Wenford Railway with excitement and anticipation.

As they say in other circles – watch this space!

Bodmin Road

The economies of both Devon and Cornwall have been dependent on tourism for much of their survival this century. Not only were long, heavily laden holiday trains a regular sight in the spring and summer months on the counties' railways in steam days, but also prestigious named expresses were promoted for the travellers to the area: the likes of the 'Cornish Riviera', 'Royal Duchy', 'Devonian' and 'Cornishman' are the stuff of legend. Here, the last named, although without headboard, pauses at Bodmin Road on 11 June 1956, behind 83G (Penzance)-allocated No 4908 *Broome Hall*, with the fireman posing for his photograph. The tall post to the left is for the pressurised oil lamps used to light the platform.

Forty-odd years later there has been much change. With the growth of trees, the whole area has a much less open feel, a point reinforced by the fencing and brick wall (right), which now extends over the end of what was a short branch to the east side of the down platform. Trackwork has been rationalised with the disappearance of the old goods shed (the line to the right *Broome Hall*), customer facilities on the station have been drastically reduced, and long-distance cross-country services are now merely two-car DMUs – but at least the ex-GWR footbridge is still extant. An attempt at glamorising these services has been made by dubbing them 'Alphaline', the logo for which can be seen on the two cars of set No 158843. Although the units are more often used on trains to South Wales from Penzance, the service seen here has a shorter run, being the 1143 Paignton-Penzance, on 30 March 1998.
Michael Mensing/MJS

A view similar to that opposite, but this time seen from the down side. Shrouded in steam that will not assist the driver's view of the road ahead, 'Castle' Class 4-6-0 No 4086 *Builth Castle* awaits to restart the 12.35am Manchester-Penzance train on 3 March 1954. The driver looks back at the station staff, awaiting the 'right away', mail sacks having been deposited on the platform. Note the sidings in the foreground, the typical GWR lower-quadrant signal and the water tower on the left, provided for the branch train to Bodmin General. The signal gantry on the up platform, with its 'sail spar' appearance, had been demolished within two years of this view.

On 31 July 1976 track rationalisation can again be judged, together with the disappearance of some station buildings, as D1001 *Western Pathfinder* pauses with the 8.30am Cardiff-Penzance train. Note that, with the advances in signalling techniques and the resultant removal of the need for locos to carry headcodes to be read by signalmen, the 'Western' has its own number in the headcode box – a practice common at this time. At this date the days of the diesel-hydraulics – only used on ex-GWR routes – were numbered. Many of the class had already been withdrawn and *Western Pathfinder* was not to last much longer, being withdrawn just four months later and cut up at Swindon Works in August 1977.

The view today, compared with 1954, is spartan indeed! Waiting shelters have been provided since 1989, but little else, as the small, privately run cafe in the old signal box is not 'open all hours'. *Peter Gray/Norman Preedy/MJS*

Looking south, we see 'Grange' Class 4-6-0 No 6837 *Forthampton Grange* leaving a hazy halo over its train as it breasts the long 1 in 65 climb and eases on to the level track through the station on 8 September 1955, at the head of the 10.05 Penzance-Liverpool cross-country express. To the left is the goods shed, its two sidings and loading gauge, while to the right are the sidings for the branch to Bodmin General and roads for shunting freight loads to and from there and on to Boscarne Junction and Wenford. Note how clean and tidy everywhere looks.

The rising gradient to the station now presents little obstacle to modern traction and passengers in DMU set No 158867, enjoying the journey of the 1145 Penzance-Cardiff Central service, would most likely not even notice any extra effort from their train. In the sunshine of 23 May 1998, the changes on both sides of the line are obvious. Cars justifying the 'Parkway' sobriquet lie to the left, while the sidings on the right now house much spare stock for the Bodmin & Wenford Railway. *Peter Gray/MJS*

The branch to Bodmin General was for long the preserve of ex-GWR '45XX' Class 2-6-2 tanks. Initially introduced by Churchward in 1906 for light branch and unhurried cross-country work, those built from 1927 onwards (numbered from 4575) were fitted with tanks giving increased water capacity. One of this later type, No 5521, of 83E (St Blazey) shed, stands in the branch platform at Bodmin Road on 10 May 1958, waiting to form the 12.20pm train to Wadebridge. In the distance can be seen the unusual design of water tower built on the embankment at the north end of the station; having to reach across the branch tracks to reach the main-line platform, water flowed via a mini-aqueduct. The tracks beneath it were later severed, preventing access to the main line from this direction. The all-over canopy covered both branch and main-line platforms, as well as the footbridge steps, and made for very reasonable waiting conditions for intending passengers.

Almost exactly 40 years later much has changed. The water tower disappeared shortly after the end of steam in Cornwall and the up platform was later extended to accommodate High Speed Trains. The canopy has gone, together with its station buildings, and only the stairway now remains, but with no shelter at this point for branch travellers. Preserved saddle tank No 62 *Ugly* waits to return a special charter train to Bodmin General in March 1998. *Brian Morrison/MJS*

Coleslogett and Bodmin General

The line westwards along the branch from Bodmin Parkway climbs steadily for over 2 miles, with the ruling gradient for much of this distance being 1 in 40. This requires some real effort with a heavy load, but on 18 April 1960 No 4559 is not unduly taxed by its two-coach load as it climbs towards the line's summit with the 4.25pm train to Bodmin General. The train has just left what is now the site of Coleslogett Halt (opened 17 April 1992) and is running close to the A38 at this point. Note the difference in tank shape to No 5521 on the previous page, No 4559 being one of the earlier engines. Its earlier vintage was also contributory to this St Blazey-allocated loco's demise, being withdrawn just five months after this view.

The tree ahead of No 4559 in the 'past' view is now part of the clump in the centre of the 'present' shot, precluding a truly exact equivalent. Much other growth over the years is obvious and only the general slope of the field gives the clue to the location. The locomotive – No 6024 *King Edward I* – and its headcode would not normally have been seen on the Bodmin branch; officially banned south of Plymouth in BR steam days, rumours abound of 'clandestine'/unofficial visits to Cornwall (even one to Penzance in about 1961!). May 1998 saw the first official trip of a 'King' over the Saltash bridge and a three-week visit to the Bodmin & Wenford. On Bank Holiday Saturday, 23 May, with its long train healthily full of passengers savouring the experience, the engine works hard up the gradient from the stop at the Halt, with the 1210 returning service from Parkway to General. *Peter Gray/MJS*

Breasting the summit near 'The Quarry', 2½ miles from the main line and on virtually level ground, No 4552 rings the changes of passenger duties by bringing a short goods train from Bodmin Road, bound for the sidings at General station at 4.25pm on 27 May 1961. With tarpaulin tightly covering the two four-wheeled wagons, the consist could well be connected with the china clay industry. The lower-water-capacity, straight-topped tanks of the earlier '45XX' design can clearly be seen in this view. Again allocated to 83E (St Blazey), No 4552 was very near the end of its life here, being withdrawn in September 1961.

Almost exactly 27 years later, on 24 May 1998, with the weather closing in after a promising start and a strong wind catching the exhaust, 'King' No 6024 is seen again, approaching 'The Quarry' with the 1410 train from Parkway, showing the curve at this point. *Peter Gray/MJS*

Very nearly at its destination, No 4565 eases past Barracks Siding, on the level, about to pass under Beacon Road bridge and into Bodmin General station, the semaphore confirming that the platform road is clear. The train, made up of the two coaches usual for the branch traffic, is the 2.30pm Bodmin Road-Wadebridge and the date is 27 May 1961, just four short months before the engine is withdrawn. The allotment on the left appears to be producing good crops and the holder has already erected his runner bean poles in readiness for vigorous growth over the next few months.

Today the allotment has gone, as have the views to the distant fields on both sides of the line. The siding is also no more, although its position can be judged from the very short stretch of track to the right. Currently only one line is used by the Bodmin & Wenford, with the former up line now providing storage for temporarily idle stock. *Peter Gray/MJS*

This delightful view from Beacon Road bridge epitomises the attraction of steam-operated 'backwater' branch lines. With plenty of time between passenger services and the china clay traffic from Wenford, no one seems in a particular hurry as No 4552 undertakes shunting manoeuvres on 27 May 1961. Much of the stock seen in the distance will be moved during the operations, before No 4552 eventually leaves with a train largely comprising the clay 'hoods' seen in the platform.

Over 45 years later the trackwork is still virtually 'as was', with only subtle differences apparent from this view. Elsewhere, however, there has been much change. The engine shed, to the left, is no more; the original water tower, goods shed and signal box have also been demolished; and the sidings to the right have seen alteration. A new signal box and water tower were erected early in 1998, as can be seen in this view, and, with the station buildings that are still extant, they serve to restore an air of past GWR practice. The coach to the left is ex-BR Mk 3 sleeping car 10618, now used as volunteer accommodation and painted maroon to 'blend in' with the local ambience. *Peter Gray/MJS*

Another superb view from this photographer on 27 May 1961, again from Beacon Road bridge, shows No 4552 restarting its two-coach load from General station and taking the line towards Boscarne Junction, forming the 12.20pm Bodmin Road-Wadebridge service. Opened in September 1888, the stretch to Boscarne is on a falling gradient from General of mostly 1 in 40/45. Although slightly unusual due to historical accident, being a terminus on a 'through' route, this view again demonstrates the allure of the branch-line scene, complete with sleepy station and single-road engine shed. *Peter Gray*

Down on ground level, more of the terminus's charm can be witnessed, as No 4584, of the later design with sloping tanks, leaves with a morning service to Bodmin Road on 3 September 1954. The signalman makes an entry in his register as the loco passes him, while the goods shed plays host to what seems to be some sort of produce van.

Two years on, in June 1956, not a lot has changed, other than more vans on the goods shed road, but we now have a clearer view of the station buildings and nameboard. Despite General station being the second terminus in the town, opened in 1887 after the Bodmin & Wadebridge Railway's Bodmin North, in true GWR style the newcomer defiantly announces itself merely as 'Bodmin', leaving the nomenclature 'General' to appear only in literature until 1949. The signal box closed together with others to Wadebridge on 17 December 1967, goods traffic at General having ceased seven months earlier.

Despite having been closed to passengers from January 1967 and only remaining on the railway map by virtue of the china clay traffic, with progressive loss of much of the original infrastructure, the efforts of the Bodmin & Wenford Railway to recreate the original are bearing fruit, as can be seen from this view in March 1998. The PW hut on the left is missing, but the company has done wonders to replicate the signal box and store room, and although the goods shed is missing, the erection of a new water tower on part of the site does much to add to the feel of it all, as do the station sign and original track layout. The original water tower, seen on page 17, is now in use at Didcot Railway Centre. *R. C. Riley/J. W. T. House, C. L. Caddy collection/MJS*

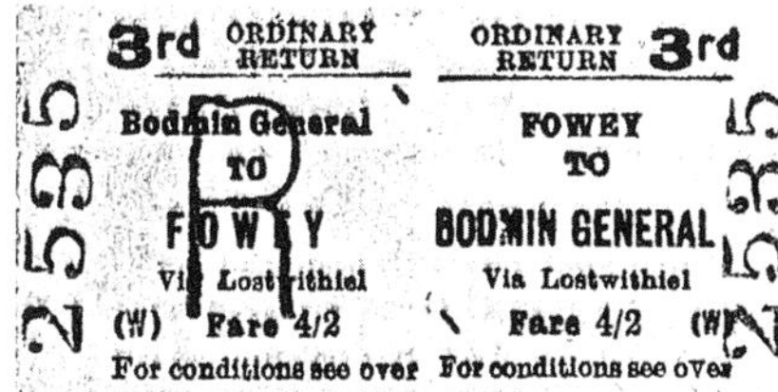

The single-road shed mentioned on page 17 is seen again here, housing No 4565 taking water between duties, as fellow class member, but of later design, No 5539 enters with the 3.24pm from Wadebridge on 18 March 1961. The fireman of No 4565 rests his foot on the water bag, to prevent spillage, as he watches the driver of the train loco prepare to hand the single-line token to the signalman as he enters the station platform. Both locomotives, allocated to St Blazey at this time, were withdrawn from stock within 12 months. Note the typical GWR dome-capped water tower and Beacon Road bridge in the background. The shed closed in April 1962.

While the two 'main lines' are intact, the old up line, occupied by locos from Classes 08 and 20 in March 1998, the trackwork and the environment around the old shed area have all changed substantially. The inspection pit still remains, but otherwise the view does not hold quite the same attraction as before. Note how the undergrowth has sprouted over the years and the view to Beacon Road bridge is now obscured by a new foot-bridge, testament to the increase in road traffic over the last 20 years or so. *Peter Gray/MJS*

Above and below left Bodmin General station was opened on 27 May 1887, connecting the county town of Cornwall with the GWR main line to London. Although undated, this typically posed view of station and engine staff is presumed to be around the turn of the century. Note the procession of period gas lamps (something for the preserved railway to recreate?), the store shed, a mixed array of freight wagons in the siding and the apparent closeness of the houses to the yard. The loco is '850' Class 0-6-0ST No 1905, built at Wolverhampton in 1881, but somewhat unusually it has had the rear bunker sheet extended upwards; the cab roof has stayed with original length, however, the gap being bridged by tarpaulin. The gentleman standing next to the engine is presumably the driver and appears to be the same man as in the accident view below.

Although the lamp standards are missing, the steps taken by the Bodmin & Wenford to recreate the past ambience are shown to good effect here. Loco No 62 *Ugly* waits to take its specially chartered party to Bodmin Parkway and back in March 1998. *Lens of Sutton/MJS*

Below right The date is August 1910 and the engine, No 1905 again, has overshot the buffer stops due to a brake failure! Note that the rear lamp bracket has moved over the years from the view above and the plant growth on the station wall has been prodigious since the first view. The enamel sign on the wall advertises 'Nectar Tea' – no doubt all concerned would appreciate some at this time! *Maurice Dart collection*

Another view from the years immediately preceding the First World War, and the importance of freight traffic to the branch can be judged from the mixture of vehicles seen in the yard, together with the animal pen to the right. To the left is the corner of the goods shed, and the wagon in front of it has been limewashed, to control infection when transporting livestock.

Eighty-odd years later the presence of motor traffic is self-evident. The entrance to the old animal pen has been walled up, with the fence now reaching to the old weighbridge. The houses to the right of and above the station canopy still survey the scene, but to the left of the latter more housing has marched along the hillside. *Lens of Sutton/MJS*

A view of the approach road to General station in the early post-war years, clearly showing the unfettered waiting area. Motor vehicles are beginning to appear in greater number and buses ply their trade to the station door. A train has presumably just arrived, judging by the souls (shoppers?) marching steadfastly down the hill. Like its Southern Railway neighbour, General station received its suffix in September 1949.

The height of the station above the road is deceptive, but can be judged by the rebuilding on the station approach, which now has a more level vista immediately outside. The road junction has been completely remodelled, as has the actual entrance to the station, with its former canopy now absent. The rather grandiose building in the left distance is the old barracks, and still holds court over the scene, now being home to the Museum of the Duke of Cornwall's Light Infantry. *Lens of Sutton/MJS*

Finally, before leaving General station, we return to Beacon Road bridge and look down the branch towards Boscarne Junction and Wadebridge, a view that became possible from 3 September 1888, when the branch to Boscarne was opened. On a sunny 10 September 1960 branch favourite No 4565 climbs the last stretch of 1 in 42, bringing the 11.35am train from Padstow into the terminus.

As seen elsewhere, growth of flora over the years has dramatically changed the appearance of many views. The very open aspect of 1960 has here been obliterated by bush and tree growth, giving the view a much less spacious feel. On 24 May 1998 No 19, the last steam loco to leave Devonport Dockyard, climbs up that same gradient with a returning freight from Boscarne Junction. *Peter Gray/MJS*

Bodmin North and Dunmere

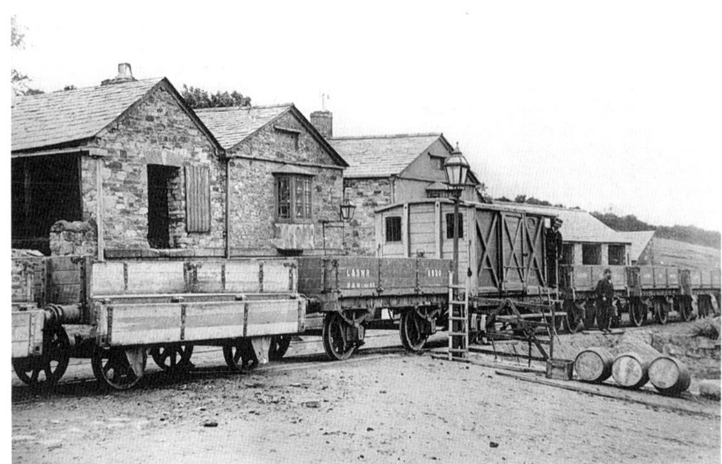

The Bodmin & Wadebridge Railway was the first to reach the town, arriving there in 1834, its main trade being transportation of sea sand from Wadebridge for use on the farmlands of the Camel valley, a function to which the notice below refers. Coal was also an important traffic. A feature of the terminus was the sand drop, over which locomotives were not allowed to work. Seen here in 1888 on the right beyond the barrels, with a delightful selection of wagons in attendance, the actual 'drop' had recently been filled in, the line now being used for other traffic. The buildings in the background, including stables and stores, were demolished in 1895 to make way for a cattle dock when the new station was being created. Note that although the LSWR absorbed the B&WR in 1846, wagon 8820 is still carries 'B&W Line 65'. Note also the gas lamps – they would not throw much light on the scene at night!

Yes, this is the same view in 1998! Only the bank to the rear gives any clue, and certainly no one would suspect that a railway had ever run here! The sand drop, roughly where the cars are parked, was filled in around 1887. *Roger Carpenter collection/MJS*

ATTENDANCE WILL BE GIVEN AT THE RAILWAY OFFICE,

ON THE WHARF AT BODMIN,

On WEDNESDAY, the 25th of January, 1871,

Also, on SATURDAY, the 28th of January, and SATURDAY, the 4th and 11th of February,

On each Day between the hours of Eleven and Five,

FOR THE PURPOSE OF RECEIVING

The AMOUNT due for SAND, on the 31st of December, 1870.

Any Accounts, not paid as above, may be settled at the OFFICE, at *Wadebridge*, on any day except the above, until the 13th of February, 1871. All Accounts, not settled on or before that day, will be handed over to the Law Clerk of the Company, and payment enforced without further notice, at the costs of the defaulters.

Bottom left A wonderful peek into a past era: note the dire warning at the end of the notice! *Roger Carpenter collection*

Opposite page A general view of North station in the early years of this century, with the site of the sand drop to the right (the gas lamp is still in position). This 'new' station, just called 'Bodmin' until September 1949, well after the opening of the GWR terminus elsewhere in the town, was built in local stone, to replace the previous Wharf facilities seen opposite. It opened in November 1895, some eight years or so after the previous passenger services had been 'temporarily' suspended! Never a bustling place, the scene seems to be the epitome of siesta time! Note the short wooden awning, to cope with the equally short normal trains, and the antiquated covered

van in the right-hand siding, with what is possibly the guard's door wide open.

The date is 24 July 1964 and British Railways is trying to cut costs on the branch from Boscarne Junction by running the service with a one-car four-wheeled railbus. The train shuttled back and forth between North station and a new exchange platform built two months earlier at Boscarne at a cost of £2,000, linking with the Bodmin General-Padstow services. The experiment was not a great success and the finale came at the end of January 1967, when all passenger services west of Bodmin Road were withdrawn and the Padstow-Wadebridge stretch was closed to all traffic. The little girl in her father's arms is perhaps seeing friends on to the 4.30pm departure and not travelling herself, as her toy dog stands by the trolley to the left of the railbus. Note the track rationalisation already completed and the grass reclaiming the area behind the buffer stops. Steam had ceased at the terminus a month earlier.

Again scarcely recognisable as the same place, the two-chimneyed house in the centre of all three shots is the clue, together with the bay-windowed bungalow just left of centre. As so often in post-Beeching days, tarmac has covered the trackbed. *Lens of Sutton/J. H. Aston, Maurice Dart collection/MJS*

8410 SOUTHERN RAILWAY. 8410
Issued subject to the Bye-laws, Regulations & Conditions in the Company's Bills and Notices.
(NO.1) RAIL MOTOR CAR (NO.1)
Nanstallon Halt to
BODMIN
THIRD CLASS Fare 6d. THIRD CLASS Fare 6d
The Passenger is requested to see this ticket punched at the time of issue
NOT TRANSFERABLE

This page Between 1905 and 1906 the LSWR built 15 rigid-framed steam railcars, each effectively a truncated steam engine and coach wrapped together within one overall bodyshell. From mid-1906 two units at a time were deployed on the Bodmin North branch, and within a couple of years of that date No 8 disgorges its complement of Edwardian businessmen and ladies from Wadebridge. The units potentially held 40 passengers, but underpowered by the tractive effort of the 'locomotive', they would have struggled over the route with a full load. Note the LSWR coal wagons on the right, fully laden with quality grade coal.

On a wet 19 August 1958, steam still rules. Ex-SR 'O2' Class No 30236 waits with the doors of carriage set 29 open, hopefully to attract custom for the 2pm train to Padstow. Note the headcode No 1, covering the route, the very healthy stock of freight wagons in the sidings and the addition of 'North' to the original sign to differentiate the station from 'newcomer' GWR at General! A long-time Wadebridge engine, No 30236 was withdrawn in January 1960.

That bungalow is seen again on the extreme left to identify the views. *Pendragon Collection/E. Wilmhurst/MJS*

Opposite page Although normally a sleepy station, there was much activity, interest and excitement on 28 August 1946 when 'West Country' Class 'Pacific' No 21C116 (later to become No 34016 after Nationalisation) made the only visit of the type to the branch, to be named *Bodmin*. In the first picture the town's mayor looks very pleased with himself, dutifully bedecked with driver's cap, as he smiles from the cab after the naming ceremony.

In the second view the local populace queue for their chance to sample the footplate, shepherded by police officers. As so often happens at these events, the weather was not kind, and, judging by the umbrellas, it is still raining; presumably the official party have retired to either a local hostelry or to the Pullman Car and Inspection Coach seen at the rear of the branch train in the distance. As to the crowd and its many young children – where are they now? *Both Southern Railway, Bodmin & Wenford collection*

Another view of the station, this time from the buffer stops and affording another glimpse of No 30236, commendably clean, arriving on Whit Monday, 18 May 1959, with the 2.56pm from Padstow. The three coaches, led by Bulleid gangway 2nd side-corridor coach S106S, appear to be ex-Works; the other two are the standard Maunsell BCK/BSK format for the branch, and it would be interesting to know why the Bulleid interloper is present. Certainly they are an unusual trio for the branch, but as they glisten in the sunshine, and boasting corridors, they would have been a good advertisement for the local service. Note the prominent tower in the left distance, belonging to Bodmin Gaol, and the delightful poster for Spillers Shapes on the platform. The two central sidings seen in the foreground were lifted in 1964, at the end of steam on the branch.

The tower remains today, as do the lineside houses, but gone is the raised vantage point of the older view, and the gas holder as well as the railway has disappeared. Somewhat surprisingly for 1998, very few television aerials have sprouted and there are no satellite dishes visible! *Michael Mensing/MJS*

Dunmere Halt was opened on 2 July 1906 by the LSWR and, isolated from any meaningful habitation, it never boasted much in the way of facilities. The spartan pagoda-style waiting room is all that stood on the single platform for the benefit of passengers, apart from the station sign and two rather primitive gas lamps. This is the view shortly before the First World War, with the path down to the platform from the A389 road overbridge coming in from the right. With the lack of station facilities, tickets were issued and collected by the train guards, as they were for Grogley and Nanstallon Halts. The climb from here to Bodmin North was largely at 1 in 47.

SOUTHERN RAILWAY.
Issued subject to the Bye-laws, Regulations & Conditions in the Company's Bills and Notices.
0146 Bodmin to 0146
Dunmere
Via
First Class Fare
NOT TRANSFERABLE

Now part of the Camel Trail, at least the platform and pathway down (just visible to the right) are still present, but other than the trackbed being kept clear by constant wear from foot and cycle, Nature is attempting reclamation! The previous open aspect is now almost a leafy tunnel. *Lens of Sutton/MJS*

Wenford branch

WENFORD MINERAL LINE.

Traffic is conveyed to and from the line by the mineral train from Wadebridge, and the Guard of this train will be responsible for the proper working of the points.

Only one engine in steam is allowed on the line at one time, and as the branch is not provided with signals, fencing or any protection, a train passing over it must be moved at such a speed that it can be stopped promptly before reaching any obstruction that may be observed on the line by the Enginemen.

Trains must pass over this line only during daylight.

Six-wheeled vehicles must not be permitted to work over this line.

From the SR General Appendices to the Working Time Tables, 1934.

At Dunmere Junction the Wenford branch diverged from the line from Boscarne Junction to Bodmin North. On 2 June 1960 Beattie Well Tank 2-4-0T No 30585 slowly moves the 10.03am freight from Wadebridge, reporting number 637, on to the 1834 freight-only Wenford tracks, with both driver and guard, carrying the branch token, posing for the photographer after safely negotiating the pointwork. The guard will have to walk back to Boscarne Junction box with the token before rejoining his train! Just out of sight behind the train and close by the telegraph pole was Dunmere Junction box, a diminutive structure that controlled the point's ground frame. The picture oozes health, with both loco and stock in fine external condition and the surrounding infrastructure all in good repair.

Just before the junction the railway crossed the River Camel, the bridge for which can be seen here. Before 1888 the route taken was across another bridge just to the left of this one (and still in existence in 1998), with the tracks then swinging in an arc to reach the junction at a point just behind the photographer. *J. H. Aston, Maurice Dart collection/MJS*

Well Tank No 30585 pauses on its journey back from Wenford on 3 July 1961. The crew sit on the low boundary wall, waiting for the guard to return from Boscarne Junction before restarting their journey. Note the gates standing ready to be closed across the tracks, enabling the route to Wenford to be worked as 'one engine in steam', and the small shed in the centre with its tracks now no longer connected to the branch. This once held the Camel permanent way wagon, which is now to be found on Bodmin General station. Originally the route to Bodmin went through the site of this hut and up over the embankment behind, now marked by the line of trees, before swinging sharp right past St Anne's Grove, to head for the town; however, the gradient on this line was found to be too severe and the new alignment was introduced from 1888. The newer right-hand route to Bodmin North climbs from here up a 1 in 50 gradient.

The second, undated, view, suspected to be from between the wars, makes for a fascinating comparison, especially in view of the foot crossing access to the nearby dwelling and the point rodding reaching right to the gate.

Both routes now form part of the Camel Trail and a small group of walkers enjoy the early spring sunshine of March 1998. The gates on the Wenford route are now closed permanently and the shed is empty (but still just standing!); the cottage to the left has seen some renovation since 1961 and has lost a chimney stack. *Terry Gough/Peter Treloar collection/MJS*

The stone cottage in the background of the lower view on page 31 is here seen in close-up, as Well Tank No 30585 makes its way up the branch with a load of open four-wheeled 10-ton wooden-bodied wagons and Conflats bound for Wenford on 22 September 1959. Perhaps somewhat surprisingly, in view of these regular but relatively short journeys, No 30585 had completed a total of 1,314,838 miles by the time of its withdrawal!

With the growth of trees and ivy, the view is altered dramatically, appearing much more closed in than before. The light reaching the cottage door and lower windows must now be much reduced! Just ahead of the walkers is the A389 Bodmin-Wadebridge road, seen with a lorry crossing downhill. *Peter Treloar/MJS*

Dunmere crossing.—Before a mineral train passes over the road from Bodmin to Wadebridge at Dunmere crossing, situated at the foot of Dunmere Hill, it must be brought to a stand and the engine whistle sounded freely. The Guard must also stand at the crossing, in good view of the roadway, and exhibit a red flag until the train has passed over the crossing, as a warning to motorists descending the hill.

From the SR General Appendices to the Working Time Tables, 1934.

The A389 is seen again on 13 July 1961 as No 30585 crosses with a short freight for Wenfordbridge, consisting of just one 10-ton and one 16-ton wagon. The travelling shunter has safely discharged his duty of seeing the train across the road and now waits to rejoin his brake-van. The two cottages in the previous views can be seen in the left distance. While freight, especially the china clay traffic, continued on this branch after other closures in 1967, the three Well Tanks ceased handling it on their withdrawal in January 1963.

Contrary to some opinions, the Camel Trail is not a public right of way. The trackbed is owned by North Cornwall District Council, who merely allow public access until the day when a decision is finally made as to whether or not to reinstate the railway – hence the short lengths of rail remaining in situ in the tarmac. Road traffic has grown over the years and this crossing is now not the leisurely place to sit and relax (see the seat in the view above), but allowing trains to once more move china clay from Wenford would remove in the region of 8,300 lorry journeys a year from the area's highly unsuitable roads. *Peter Gray/MJS*

Just three days prior to the train on the opposite page, No 30585 is again on duty and waits here as the points to Dunmere Wharf siding are clipped in position. Immediately behind the photographer in the view opposite, the siding was of short length, originally known as 'Borough Bounds Wharf' and serving Hawke's Mill; it closed on 14 May 1969 and was lifted six months later. Not in everyday use and ending close to the road, the points remained locked in the normal running position unless required by the train crew. A shunting pole lies on the ground to the right, evidence that manoeuvres have just been undertaken.

The Camel Trail marches north-eastward, with the concrete slabs of the fence on the left still marking the boundary and the fence-line on the right replacing that from 1961. Grass and weeds have encroached over the years, however, leading to the appearance of a much narrower trackway that previously. *R. C. Riley/MJS*

The hamlet of Hellandbridge is in a delightful spot on the narrow Helland-Tredethy road, at the foot of a steeply sided valley, bisected by both railway and River Camel. In summer, in the sunshine, the spot is extremely attractive, as can be seen from this view of No 30585 approaching the road crossing with a short freight from Wenford on 13 July 1961. Helland Wharf siding stood just to the right of the locomotive and was closed on 2 May 1960.

Once again, the railway tracks still linger in the tarmac as a sort of defiant token of resistance to the line's closure. Feelings are mixed locally at the thought of the railway's reinstatement, but a majority appear to be in favour, a point to be savoured by enthusiasts and ecologists alike. *Peter Gray/MJS*

To reach Hellandbridge the railway passes Pencarrow Woods, and the proximity of the River Camel is put to good use, with an opportunity for watering locomotives midway through their climb to Wenford. Not unlike the arrangement at Bodmin Road, an unusual design of water tower was installed, whereby the water ran along a metal trough before reaching the engines by more conventional bag, albeit slightly lower than the loco filler cap. The set-up can clearly be seen here, with the fireman watching the procedure, legs straddling loco and tower. Once more on duty 637, No 30585 has its thirst quenched in May 1959 while working its mixed freight up to Wenfordbridge. *Maurice Dart collection*

As on many such 'obscure' branch lines, railway society trips were not unknown. On 31 May 1958 the Plymouth Railway Circle ran a brake-van special up the branch, hauled by No 30587, proudly displaying its 72F (Wadebridge) shedplate. Here the train is restarted from the water stop, with the legs of the water tower just visible level with the third brake-van. *Peter Gray*

After leaving Dunmere the line remained single, often closely hemmed in by trees or cuttings, until it reached Tresarrett Wharf, where a slightly flatter topography and the presence of a mill gave rise to further sidings. In June 1960 No 30587 shunts a long train, including a mixture of wagons, Conflats and a perishables van; some of the stock has been placed in the siding, perhaps to alleviate shunting problems at Wenford, just a mile or so further north. The siding on which the loco stands was closed in July 1970, being lifted the following year.

Looking at the site today, there hardly seems enough width or length to accommodate the train seen above, but the encroachment of vegetation makes appearances deceptive. Certainly the brambles do their best to ensnare any photographer attempting to recreate the past! *Harry Cowan, Maurice Dart collection/MJS*

From the SR General Appendices to the Working Time Tables, 1934.

Tresarrett Quarry Co's siding.—A scotch block is provided on the siding side of the gate.

The men in charge of the mineral train before using the siding must be careful to remove the scotch block from the rail, close the catch points and secure them in that position by padlock whilst shunting is in progress, and when the work has been completed the points must be returned to their normal position and re-locked.

Vehicles for the siding must be placed immediately behind the scotch block in the siding, and those from the siding must be accepted at that point.

The responsibility for the movement of vehicles over the siding beyond the Company's boundary will rest with the Tresarrett Quarry Company, and in no circumstances must the Company's engine pass beyond the exchange point referred to.

Wagons higher than 9 feet above rail must not be permitted to pass under the loading bins at this siding.

The Wenford Dries plant of English China Clays was the major destination for the branch from Boscarne Junction, some 6 miles away. On 22 July 1958 No 30585 is seen again, having just made its lunchtime arrival at the clay sidings with its empty stock load from the 10am from Wadebridge, this time as duty 607. The box vans will receive a complement of bagged clay before their return down the branch. The clay originates in 'liquid' form from Stannon Moor, some 6 miles distant, and arrives at the drying plant by pipeline.

After the demise of steam on the branch, the haulage up to Wenford was taken over by diesel shunters, 350hp Class 08s after the failure of trials with 03s. In 1978 the duty has fallen to No 08113, and it is seen here, having deposited its upward load, undertaking shunting tasks before returning down the branch. A tarpaulin covers the wagon to protect against china clay dust pervading everything around it! No 08113 was still around five years later to run the last day's services, on 26 September 1983. Built at the BR Works in Derby in 1955 as D3179, and first allocated to the shed in that town, it received its TOPS number of 08113 in April 1974. Having travelled widely, it finally saw BR use at Cardiff, from where it was withdrawn in March 1984 and sold on to an open cast mining concern at Gwaun-Cae-Gurwen. The space between the tracks once held a further set of rails.

As stated above, the clay freight trips from Wenford, originally to Wadebridge/Padstow, then Fowey, ceased in September 1983, after a 121-year history, following which the whole line was closed. Lorry transportation took over, but the tracks at Wenford Dries were not ripped up wholesale. Evidence of their presence can still just be seen beyond the swathe of grass, and this will aid greatly in the reinstatement of rail, should the wishes of English China Clays, the Bodmin & Wenford Railway and others come to fruition. *Terry Gough/Graham Roose/MJS*

The tall exhaust chimneys of the furnaces at the Clay Dries dominate the scene at Wenford as No 30585 shunts stock on 22 September 1959. The driver of duty 637 rests easily on his cabside, as a shunter calls him on; note the bucket and ash shovel fixed to the tank rear. The box vans will be filled with top-quality bagged clay.

Over the years the chimneys have been reduced in height and, with what looks to be plant growth from the top of one of them, they are presumably no longer in use in 1998. The track on which No 30585 stood is no longer in situ, but those behind still remain, ready for that possible re-use. *Peter Treloar/MJS*

From the SR General Appendices to the Working Time Tables, 1934.

English China Clay Company's siding.—This siding has connections to the Wenford line at either end, and two other connections about midway in the siding.

The men in charge of the mineral train when using the siding must be careful to close the catch point at the Wenford end and secure it in that position by padlock whilst shunting is in progress at that end of the siding, and when the work has been completed, all the points leading from the siding must be locked in position to prevent vehicles running foul of the main line.

The half a mile or so from Wenford to Wenfordbridge initially started as double track, as can be seen in this view of No 30585, yet again, as it starts its train of five fitted vans away from the Dries sidings on 3 July 1961.

A prize for anyone who would have guessed this to be the same spot! Maurice Dart, long-time supporter of the Bodmin & Wenford preserved railway, stands roughly where the right-hand front buffer of No 30585 was, but there are no tracks remaining here and no evidence of there ever having been a railway. *Terry Gough/MJS*

Midway to the final destination, the ubiquitous No 30585 indulges in some rather lazy shunting on 3 July 1961. The van behind the loco is coupled, but the others are being loose shunted, making use of the ruling 1 in 147 falling gradient, eventually to be pushed into the Wenfordbridge yard. The branch was truncated to roughly this point in 1971. The delightful countryside of the area can be well judged from this angle.

Again, Nature is attempting to re-establish control and only the positioning of 'human interest' in 1998 pinpoints the spot where No 30585 stood. *Terry Gough/MJS*

On a bright sunny 22 September 1959, No 30585, once more on duty 637, has marshalled a train of ten china clay wagons and two vans at Wenford and, duly tarpaulined, has brought them forward to Wenfordbridge for final shunting manoeuvres, before returning down the branch. Wenfordbridge was the furthest point from Waterloo on the Southern Railway!

By 1998 road vehicles have made tracks that deceive when trying to judge the old rail alignment. The hill in the distance and the left-hand fence line confirm the location, however. *Peter Treloar/MJS*

Below **From the SR General Appendices to the Working Time Tables, 1934.**

Wenford Bridge terminus.—There are several sidings at this terminus with points leading into them facing for trains approaching from Boscarne Junction.

A single tongue runaway catch point, facing for trains from Wenford, exists in the single line about ¼ mile from Wenford Bridge terminus, which is normally left open and secured in that position by padlock, the key of which is kept by the Guard of the mineral train.

The Driver of a mineral train must be careful to stop before reaching this catch point, and the Guard must unlock and close the point to admit of the train passing over it safely, afterwards re-locking it in its normal position.

Looking in the opposite direction, towards the end of the tracks at Wenfordbridge, No 30585 shunts stock for duty 607 under the 5-ton loading crane gantry on 2 July 1958. In the consist are china clay wagons, box vans and Conflats, a real mixture for this isolated railhead. To the right are scales for weighing out measures of coal from the yard's stocks. The gantry was erected mainly for loading timber and was not in everyday use, with inwards traffic being of coal and fertiliser. Freight traffic ceased from 13 February 1967.

The coalyard continued for some time after the disappearance of the railway, but by 1998 it had closed and dereliction was more the order of the day. The Austin A40 is dumped and coal ash litters the yard. *Terry Gough/MJS*

Another view of No 30585 under the gantry in happier times. On 19 July 1960 a 16-ton steel-bodied wagon accompanies the more usual fare for the branch, completing a delightful portrait of the locomotive, complete with fire irons and rubber bucket. *R. C. Riley*

The final view at Wenfordbridge is in the days when the tracks actually went even further into the hinterland, eventually finishing up at T. W. Ward & Sons' quarry at De Lank, half a mile or so to the north. Looking south towards Wenford around the turn of the century, with the quarry line behind the photographer, a De Lank train loaded with granite blocks stands in Wenfordbridge yard awaiting the off, hauled by an unidentified tank engine, while the guard and driver pose for the camera. Quarry traffic, hauled up and down the steep 1 in 8 incline by means of a cable, ceased in the early years of the last war, although official closure was not until 1950.

The high vantage point no longer available, this is the 1998 comparative view, with that car again and the remains of a coal bunker to the left. *Maurice Dart collection/MJS*

Boscarne to Grogley

The 1 in 45 gradient up from Boscarne Junction towards Bodmin meant that steam engines, especially, had to work hard, even with relatively short trains. As has already been seen, china clay trains were very important for the branch and the '45XX' tanks took their part in moving these. On 27 May 1961 No 4552 makes that climb with a second load of eight wagons, each of which has obviously seen much use on these trains!

Happily, apart from the proliferation of local flora, there has been very little change in the area and this short freight on the preserved line, seen on 23 May 1998, recreates the above scene very well, even down to the 83E (St Blazey) shedplate. The Bodmin & Wenford had recently cleared much of the left-hand embankment, making this view possible. *Peter Gray/MJS*

Just around the curve from the view on the previous page the line runs into the junction proper. Becoming a junction in 1888, when the GWR line from Bodmin General met the existing route to Wenford, it saw passenger services until 1967. For the last three years an Exchange Platform was constructed to give an easy physical connection between the two branch routes. The diminutive wooden structure, costing some £2,000, can be seen here on 11 June 1966, looking towards Bodmin General and viewed from a brake-van taking the Wenford route. The platform boasted two gas lamps and a sign board almost as big as itself! Note the distinctive lattice signal post, with arms controlling both directions and the hut controlling the ground frame. The point and signal rodding can be seen running between the hut and the platform.

Signs of previous occupation can be seen from the telegraph boxes, but otherwise it is impossible to judge that a station had been here. In 1998 the remains of a signal post – sadly, not the lattice one – is still in position roughly where the old one stood. *C. L. Caddy/MJS*

The exchange facilities set up in June 1964 are seen here on 24 July of that year. On the right, single-car DMU No W55001 has arrived from Bodmin General and pauses at the platform for any passengers to alight or board; the semaphore signals the road clear to proceed towards Wadebridge. To the left, the road ahead denied by the tall LSWR lattice-post signal, a four-wheeled railbus – No W79977, capable of carrying 50 passengers! – waits for business before returning to Bodmin North, with tall metal steps giving access from the trackbed. The driver of this railbus looks less than excited by the whole arrangement! Note the newly installed oil lamps ready to light the way along the very short path between stops. The station signboard proudly announces 'Boscarne Junction. Change for Dunmere & Bodmin North'.

Apart from the track, two signal posts and the stems of the gas lamps mark this as being the same spot in 1998. The trackbed to the left leads into the Camel Trail, but all this could come back to life if the proposals for re-instatement of the china clay traffic succeed. *J. H. Aston, Maurice Dart collection/MJS*

Table 97 BODMIN ROAD, BODMIN GENERAL, WADEBRIDGE and PADSTOW

WEEK DAYS ONLY (Z)

Miles from Bodmin Road	Miles from Bodmin Nth		am B		am		am V		am	am	am		am			am V	am		am	pm	pm	pm
		Bodmin Road .. .. dep	6 55				7 50						9 5			10 5				1220		1 32
3½		**Bodmin Gen.** ¶.. arr	7 8				7 58						9 13			1013				1228		1 40
		dep			7 27		8 8				8 58					1020				1238		
—		**Bodmin North** dep							8 43								1120					
—	1½	Dunmere Halt							8 47								1124					
6½	2¼	Nanstallon Halt			7 34		8 15		8 50								1127			1245		
8	3¾	Grogley Halt			7 39				8 54								1131					
11	6¾	**Wadebridge** .. arr			7 48		8 27		9 2		9 16					1037	1139			1257		
		dep			7 50		8 40			9 12						1039			1158		1 15	
16½	12¼	**Padstow** ...... arr			8 0		8 50			9 22						1049			12 9		1 29	

	pm		pm		pm	pm X	pm T	pm	pm		pm	pm V		pm		pm	pm	pm	pm	pm		
Bodmin Road .. .. dep			2 30			4 25	4 35					6 15				7 0	8 0	9 5		10 5		
Bodmin Gen. ¶.. arr			2 38			4 33	4 43					6 25				7 8	8 8	9 13		1013		
dep			2 48			4 50	4 50					6 35					8 20		9 22			
Bodmin North dep	2 0				4 23				5 44													
Dunmere Halt	2 4				4 27				5 48													
Nanstallon Halt	2 7				4 30	4 57	4 57		5 51			6 42					8 28		9 30			
Grogley Halt	2 11				4 34				5 55			6 47					8 32		9 34			
Wadebridge .. arr	2 19		3 5		4 42	5 9	5 9		6 3			6 55					8 40		9 42			
dep	2 23				4 44			5 11			6 13	6 58		7 48					9 44			
Padstow ...... arr	2 34				4 55			5 21			6 22	7 9		7 58					9 54			

Miles	Miles		am	am		am	am		am	am		am	am V		am		am V		pm	pm		pm
		Padstow .. .. dep							8 12	8 30			9 3				1057					1258
5½	5½	**Wadebridge** .. arr							8 21	8 39			9 12				11 6					1 7
		dep	6 58			7 58			8 30				9 16		9 50		11 8		1225			
8½	8½	Grogley Halt	7 6			8 6			8 38						9 58				1233			
10	10	Nanstallon Halt . ..	7 10			8 10			8 42				9 30		10 2		1121		1237			
—	10¾	Dunmere Halt				8 14									10 6				1241			
—	12¼	**Bodmin North**. arr				8 18									1010				1245			
13	—	**Bodmin Gen.** ¶.. arr	7 20						8 53				9 40				1131					
		dep		7 30			8 42					9 20	9 45				1140			1 5		
16½	—	**Bodmin Road** .. .. arr		7 37			8 49					9 27	9 52				1147			1 12		

	pm		pm		pm		pm	pm	pm	pm	pm		pm		pm	pm	pm	pm	pm	pm	pm	
Padstow .. .. dep			2 52		3 13			5 2			6 0					7 35		8 30			10 5	
Wadebridge .. arr			3 1		3 22			5 11			6 9					7 44		8 39			1014	
dep	1 25		3 8				3 24	5 12		5 34			6 12			7 53			8 55			
Grogley Halt	1 33		3 17					5 21					6 20			8 3						
Nanstallon Halt . ..	1 37		3 21					5 25		5 46			6 24			8 7			9 7			
Dunmere Halt			3 25					5 29														
Bodmin North. arr			3 29					5 33														
Bodmin Gen. ¶.. arr	1 47						3 44			5 56			6 33			8 17			9 17			
dep	1 55						3 54		5 45	6 1			6 43		7 38		8 40			9 30		
Bodmin Road .. .. arr	2 2						4 1		5 52	6 8			6 50		7 45		8 47			9 37		

¶ 1 mile to Bodmin North Station
B Runs 23rd December, 1961 and Saturdays commencing 19th May, 1962
T Runs until 30th September, 1961 and commencing 16th April, 1962

V Through Train between Bodmin Road and Padstow
X Runs 2nd October, 1961 to 14th April, inclusive 1962

Z On Sundays passengers holding through rail tickets may travel by Southern National Omnibus between Bodmin Road and Wadebridge or vice versa—see Table 21

Unfortunately the exchange arrangements came too late for the Summer 1964 public timetable, which still advertised through services from North to Wadebridge.

Swinging round virtually 360 degrees, this is the view towards Wadebridge and Padstow on 3 July 1961. No 4694 has just taken the Wenford branch tracks and hurries the 2.52pm Padstow-Bodmin North train, formed of Maunsell set No 27, towards its destination. Allocated to 72F (Wadebridge), No 4694 subsequently moved to 72A (Exmouth Junction) from where it was withdrawn in 1965, when that shed was closed to steam. The appearance of the four tracks is deceptive, as all were worked as separate, independent single lines.

Looking for all the world as authentic, complete with 72F shedplate, No 1369 hauls a short freight at virtually the same spot. Appearances are deceptive, however, as the date is September 1996 and the locomotive was withdrawn (from Wadebridge) in November 1964! Just one example of what can be achieved towards reality in preservation.

In 1996 the Bodmin & Wenford Railway extended its passenger potential to Boscarne Junction and opened a single-platform station there on 14 August. Still looking new and without waiting shelter in 1998, the construction is mostly complete and will serve the railway well in years to come, either as a terminus or port of call if further extensions take place. To achieve this restoration of services, some 260 sleepers were replaced, all materials brought in by rail and all work carried out by volunteers. *Terry Gough/Anthony Clay/MJS*

In the view of No 4694 on the opposite page, the Junction signal box can just be seen to the extreme left. Here it is in close-up, as No 30585 waits for the road to Wenford and the relevant token, with its load of Conflats, on duty 637 on 22 September 1959. The box contained 14 levers and controlled the routes to Bodmin General, Bodmin North and the Dunmere Crossing connection to Wenford. Single-line tablets for the various branches were exchanged here and the basic day consisted of 15 hours duty – 0640-2145 – split between two shifts. The points mark the meeting of GWR and SR tracks; those behind the train, westwards to Wadebridge, closed on 17 December 1978.

Almost unrecognisable as the same spot, the short length of track, the metal lintel in the embankment, right of centre, and the concrete post just beyond it confirm the location. The restructuring of the landscape has been so comprehensive that it seems impossible that a signal box or any other structure ever stood here. Note the growth of trees along the route of the Trail. *Peter Treloar/MJS*

The present Boscarne Junction station is close to the village of Nanstallon, but there was no such Junction station in pre-preservation days, apart from the short-lived Exchange Platform, so the nearest facility was at Nanstallon Halt. The Halt was opened in 1906, to coincide with the introduction of steam railmotor trains on the route, but was a mile or so from the village and across the River Camel, so intending passengers had to climb a steep hill up a narrow country road to reach it. This is the original 1906 station, a simple affair with short wooden platform, no lights or waiting shelter and plain wire fence. The steep road crosses the line at the end of the platform, hence the need for signals and signal box; the splitting distant signals are well in advance of the parting of the ways at Boscarne Junction. Incredibly, despite its isolation, there was a goods siding here until 2 May 1960, situated to the left of this view, past the level crossing.

Later into the 20th century the changes are many and obvious. The platform is now concrete-based and the pagoda has a brick base; the trees have grown apace and the signal gantry has lost one of its distant arms. In common with those at Wadebridge, the signal box was closed on 17 December 1967.

Again bereft of platform structure in 1998, natural growth threatens to overwhelm both station and trackbed, and only its use as the Camel Trail keeps the latter clear. The house seen in the two 'past' views is just visible in the distance through the trees. *Lens of Sutton (2)/MJS*

Obviously the isolation of the Halt was no obstacle to patronage in this view from the late 1940s/early 1950s, judging by the number waiting to board the train. Note the pagoda-style corrugated iron waiting shelter – similar to that at Dunmere Halt – the gas lamps and the steps to help those experiencing difficulty in boarding from the slightly low platform. The gradient post shows the change in slope here, from 1 in 440 towards Wadebridge to 1 in 50 up to Boscarne Junction.

The line of the platform edging seems to have lost its shape over the years, perhaps due to the hedging and tree planted on the previous platform area. The building is not an extension of the pagoda, but a much newer edifice, serving the area behind the hedge. The Camel Trail runs on the trackbed to the right. *Lens of Sutton/MJS*

Actually designated Polbrock on an OS map, the site of Grogley Halt, a little over 2 miles from Wadebridge, was even more isolated than Nanstallon, with no inhabitation of any size nearby. Indeed, when the original structure opened on 1 June 1906, it was to serve farms and cottages nearby; it was not given lighting and trains were not allowed to stop after dark! On 10 September 1960 No 30200 makes a delightful sight running alongside the River Camel on the approach to the Halt with the 5.11pm Wadebridge to Bodmin North (4.40pm from Padstow) train. Two Maunsell side-corridor coaches provide the stock, this time of set No 196, and their occupants are obviously enjoying both the sunshine and the extremely attractive views along the valley. Not long after this view No 30200 was transferred to Plymouth Friary shed, from where it was withdrawn in August 1962. Although Polgeel House and neighbouring cottage are still extant, this view is now impossible because of the growth of vegetation, although the trackbed still remains, once again as the Camel Trail. *Peter Gray*

VIEW OF THE OPENING OF THE BODMIN AND WADEBRIDGE RAILWAY.

This lithograph was produced to depict the first train over the Bodmin & Wadebridge Railway on 30 September 1834. It shows the 'Camel Engine' hauling '22 carriages containing more than 400 persons' speeding over Pendavey bridge at some 7/8mph. There is a gentleman sitting on the front buffer beam (to chase away stray cows, etc!), one coach and a mixture of wagons, and a distinct exercise of artistic licence in both the representation of the bridge and the boat supposedly having sailed beneath it!

Just how much licence has been employed can be judged from this 1882 view. The width of the spans, actually 27 feet, and the height of the track above the central pier expose the grandiose nature of the early illustration and the extent of the artist's imagination. The original bridge was severely damaged by floods on 16 July 1847 and whether the right-hand wooden support to the decking dates from this event is unknown, but certainly the water level is rather low.

The original bridge was replaced by the LSWR with a cast-iron structure in 1887, utilising the original stone abutments and central pier and looking much more serviceable than its predecessor. Evidence of widening and deepening of the river – at the time of the new bridge? – is evident from this 1998 view. As the cyclist demonstrates, the Camel Trail runs over here at present, but the Bodmin & Wenford would very much like to return the stretch to steel rails. *Peter Treloar collection/Roger Carpenter collection/MJS*

Wadebridge

Running westwards from Pendavey Bridge, the old route very shortly joined that from Launceston through north Cornwall, and after 1907 the two ran as single lines side by side into Wadebridge, almost exactly midway between Bodmin and Padstow. This LSWR route from Waterloo reached here in 1895, 13 years after the authorising Act of Parliament, and can be seen to the right of the '45XX' approaching its destination with a train from Bodmin Road on 1 July 1961. The SR gantry gives a clear road into the station, with the outskirts of the town seen across the river. Note the 'Bodmin Road' destination board just to the right of the 1st Class compartment door.

The 'present' view is not quite from the same vantage point, but short of employing a chain-saw the elevation of the 'past' view is now impossible. Trees and undergrowth across the valley, coupled with housing and other development both in the valley bottom and on the hillside opposite, make for a deceptive comparison. There is no evidence remaining of the signal gantry or its site. *Terry Gough/MJS*

281
Great Western Railway
One Bicycle accompanied by Passenger
At Company's limited risk rate.
See Conditions on back.
TRURO TO
WADEBRIDGE
Via BODMIN ROAD
CARRIAGE PAID 1/0
This ticket which is available for a single Journey only must be given up at destination Station
281

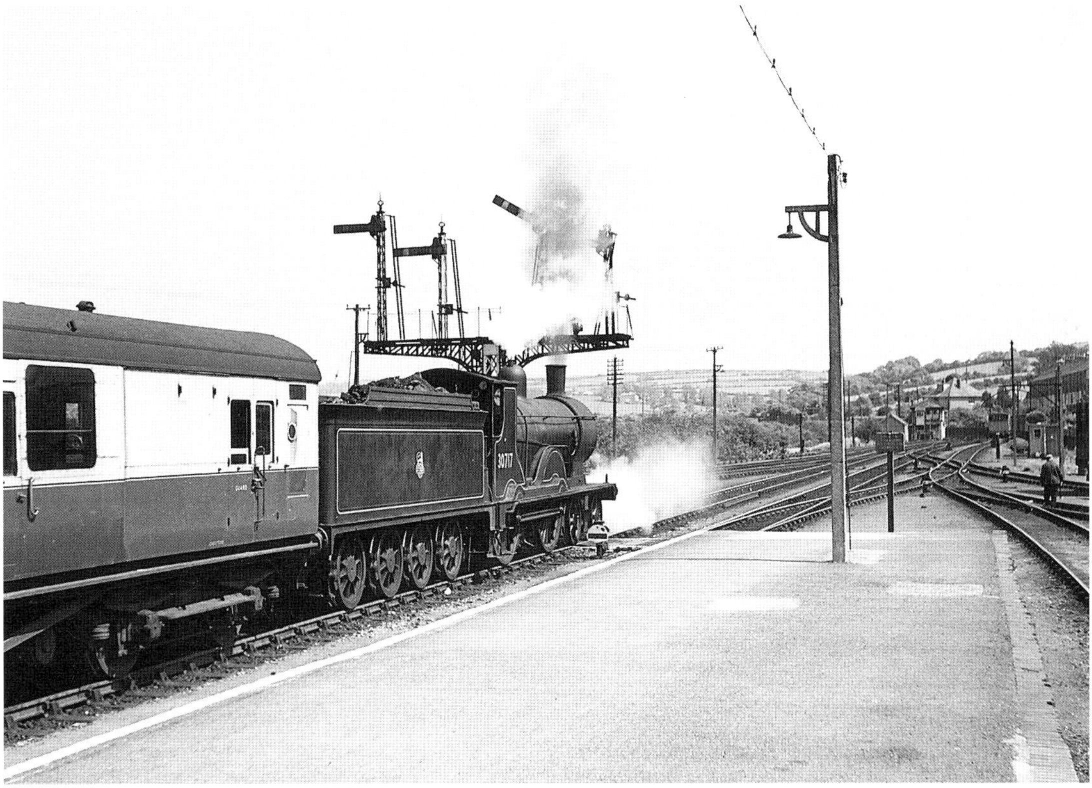

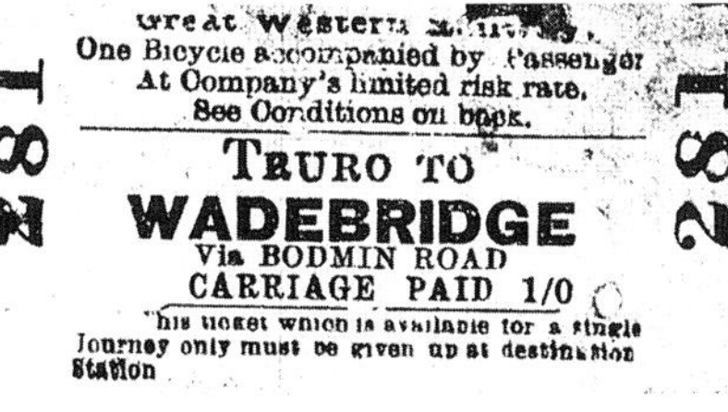

At the east end of Wadebridge station, looking towards Bodmin, a commendably clean No 30717 lets off steam from the cylinders and slips slightly as it restarts the 2.55pm Padstow-Exeter (Central) service on a sunny 11 June 1956. Note the eight-wheeled tender, a feature of the 'T9' Class, the typical SR concrete lamp standard and the 1931-vintage semaphore signal gantry. To the left are the tracks to the engine shed, while those to the right approach the goods shed and yard. In the distance can be seen the East signal box, opened in 1906 and containing 37 operational levers; this closed, in company with the West box, on 17 December 1967. As well as the routes into Wadebridge from the east, it also controlled the station and loco shed sidings.

While the trackbed for most of the route from Padstow to Bodmin currently acts as the Camel Trail, there are some deviations as it passes through Wadebridge. Part of the cause of this is the relatively new Guineaport Parc housing development constructed on the site of the station and engine shed, and the results are seen here. Despite appearances, this is the same view as above! *Michael Mensing/MJS*

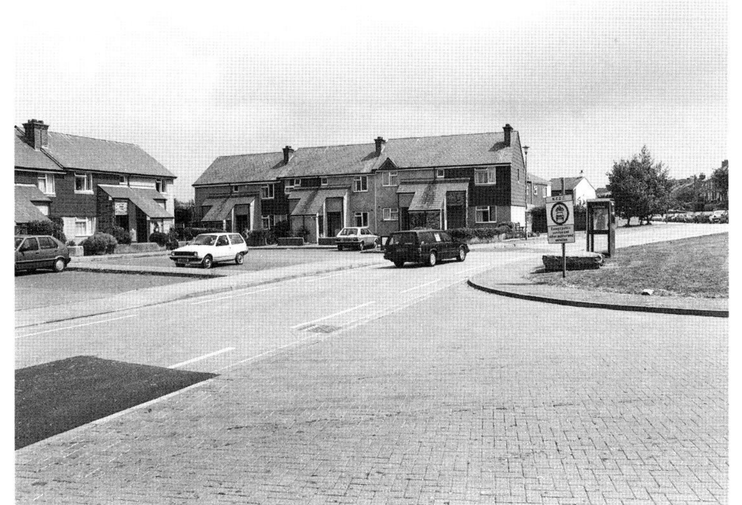

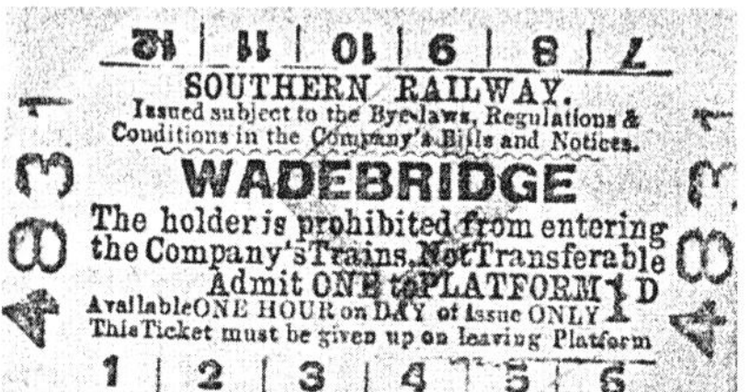

These four comparative views show development over a wide span of years. From the mid to late years of Queen Victoria's reign we see the station still with just one platform and the whole area having a very open feel. The two-road engine shed is to the right, although unoccupied in this photograph, while to the left the signal box has the town name in individual letters rather than on a board. The goods shed is situated between the signal box and the platform canopy. As the Bodmin & Wadebridge Railway opened in July 1834, the station had the distinction of being one of the first in the country, surviving with just this one platform until 1895, when an island platform was added. This gave much better operating provision to accommodate the North Cornwall route to the town, opened that year, and the Padstow extension four years later.

The date of the second view is 10 May 1958, and No 5521 leaves with the 9.03am Padstow-Bodmin Road service,

partly obscuring the 1931 signal gantry. Substantial development from the previous view is obvious, with the 1899 island platform having appeared, together with a concrete overbridge to connect to the old platform, replacing the original wooden one, and a canopy to match the original. The engine shed still stands to the right, with an extension, but the original signal box was demolished in 1899, control being transferred to two new ones. Coach set 198 waits in the north face of the island platform, later to be used for a train to Bodmin North.

Initially, in many instances demolition and redevelopment of railway property did not begin immediately after the end of services. Such was the position at Wadebridge, as this view on 10 September 1980 shows, over 13 years after passenger trains ceased, although some small industrial usage has begun at the far end. The tracks towards Padstow were lifted almost immediately, but the line to Boscarne Junction had remained open for freight until 4 September 1978.

By 1998 the change is dramatic. Happily, the old goods shed – home to the Betty Fisher Centre – and station building, complete with canopy, have been retained, although now surrounded by the housing development, but sadly the new layout precludes a railway again running along the old course. *Lens of Sutton/Brian Morrison/Graham Roose/MJS*

In this 1949 view the station is a hive of activity. Although a year into Nationalisation, Well Tank No 3314 still bears its old number and the 'Southern' legend on its splasher, as it prepares a truly mixed freight. The loco is presumably merely handling the shunting of the train, as the third vehicle, the brake-van, still bears the trains' rear lamp, which would need to be removed before leaving the station. The rest of the consist includes wagons, vans, oil wagons and even two coaches, so this could be a shipment for transmission to Bodmin General, for re-marshalling at that point. Two wooden-bodied coal wagons – one from Charringtons – wait on the right for their contents to be emptied on to the conveyor seen just past them. Arriving in the area late in Queen Victoria's reign, No 3314 was eventually to become No 30585, staying at Wadebridge until withdrawal in January 1963.

The second, similar, photograph, taken during the morning of 22 September 1959, exudes a whole different atmosphere. Despite the presence of No 30587 and its brake-van on the left, the emphasis is on passenger turns. On the near tracks a box van makes up the rear of a train to Padstow, while in the centre a very grimy 'West Country' 'Pacific' No 34033 *Chard* waits to restart the two-coach portion of the 'Atlantic Coast Express' on its long journey to Waterloo. On the right No 30199 waits with its two Maunsell coaches of set 23 on the service to Bodmin North. The 'Pacific' bears disc-code 15, covering the route between Padstow and Exmouth Junction.

Today the view is definitely not of much interest to railway enthusiasts! There is pleasant enough housing and redevelopment of the station buildings, but character and ambience have been lost. *Arthur Mace, Milepost 92½ collection/Peter Treloar/MJS*

London and South Western Ry.

787

FROM WATERLOO TO

WADEBRIDGE

Looking across to the previous vantage point and beyond, we see No 30586 on 1 July 1961, participating in a little fly shunting by the cattle dock, the shunter's pole about to release the 13-ton wagon from its coupling to the brake-van. A healthy rake of box vans sits on the goods shed road, while nearer the camera signs of track renewal are apparent from the discarded sleepers. Of the three Beattie Well Tanks stationed at Wadebridge, No 30586 was unusual in being the only one with square splashers – compare with the curves of No 30585 on page 63.

The road alongside the old station site remains in situ, as do the houses beyond and the goods shed, but it is hard to visualise there ever having been a railway here from the rest of the view, seen in May 1998. *Terry Gough/MJS*

Below **From the SR General Appendices to the Working Time Tables, 1934.**

WADEBRIDGE.

Cattle dock.—Bogie coaches must not be shunted into the cattle dock siding.

Sand Dock siding and lift bridge.—This siding is connected with one of the sidings at the west end of Wadebridge station and is extended alongside the sand dock.

A lift bridge is provided at the eastern end of the sand dock. This bridge is fitted with a locking bolt operated by a hand lever and, before movements are made over the siding leading to the sand dock, care must be taken to see that the bridge is in its proper position and is secured by the locking bolt.

The bridge has to be lifted manually with the assistance of balance weights suspended on chains, and when it is necessary for barges to pass into or out of the sand dock the bridge must be lifted sufficiently clear to enable such vessels to pass under it.

When high tides are expected care must be taken to leave the bridge unlocked in order to admit of it being automatically lifted by the rising tide, and the Station Foreman when on duty, or other member of the staff deputed by the Station Master, will be held responsible for satisfying himself that this duty has been attended to.

This view, looking westwards towards Padstow, shows the island platform usually served by Bodmin North trains and, on the right, the engine shed, coded 72F by British Railways. The 1908 wooden extension to the shed can clearly be seen beyond the 16-ton mineral wagon, and on the extreme right is the roof of the coaling stage, erected as late as 1949. No 5564, of the later design with sloping tanks, stands deceptively in tune with the peaceful air of the whole scene, as it waits with just 1 minute to go before leaving with the 1.23pm to Bodmin Road. The date is 30 June 1960 and No 5564 is one of St Blazey's stud, but the loco did not end its days in Cornwall, subsequently travelling north-east to London to be finally withdrawn from 81C (Southall) in December 1964. *David Holmes*

Being the confluence of two routes, the beneficiary of many freight workings and the domicile of local shunting locos, Wadebridge saw a wide variety of locomotive types over the years, mostly from SR and GWR stock. The engine shed could either be empty or home to a handful of visitors, as here, on 1 July 1961, where 'locals' Nos 30585/7 and 4694 play host to two SR Class 'Ns'. Steam workings having ceased on 2 January 1965, the shed building was demolished in 1969. *Terry Gough*

On 21 June 1962 No 31875, in the centre background, has worked a special into Wadebridge, while on the right signs of a new regime are manifested by the appearance of No 1368. The previously mentioned roof for the coaling stage can be clearly seen. Due to the isolated nature of the depot, and either lack of space for holding spares, or their sheer unavailability, staff had to maintain their locomotive fleet as best they could. The eastern end of the depot boasted a hoist, but this was virtually the only major appliance to hand, occasionally resulting in some improvisation to achieve repairs. Additionally, most engine coal was hand-loaded, despite there being a small hoist available! The shunter on the right seems resigned to waiting until the photographer has been satisfied! The original B&WR shed was to the west of the level crossing, this newer one appearing around 1895. *R. C. Riley*

Two days later all three Well Tanks are on view and positioned, right to left, in numerical order! Concern at their great age and thoughts that alternative motive power could handle the work with greater efficiency caused the trio to be progressively replaced during the late spring/early summer of 1962 by three ex-GWR 0-6-0Ts, numbered 1367/8 and 9. The Well Tanks were all withdrawn in January 1963, but the replacements, themselves displaced from Weymouth Quay, did not last a great deal longer, all going in October/November 1964. No 1369 became the last 'official' steam locomotive to leave Cornwall, making its way to restoration at Totnes under its own steam on 20 February 1965. In the background major work is under way on the river bank. *R. C. Riley*

On 1 July 1961 three Class 'Ns' simmer in the shed yard, making a total presence of eight locos and well worth a spotter's visit! Class members Nos 31831 and 31834 both bear the Padstow-Exeter Central disc code and appear ready to go, the former showing working 527 on its disc, while No 31857 seems to be out of steam – possibly held for some attention. Locos working over the North Cornwall route to Wadebridge were usually allocated to 72A (Exmouth Junction), a fact confirmed by these three engines. Note the liberal sprinkling of ash and coal dust around the yard, and the wheelbarrow containing yet more ash and clinker.

Can this really be the same view? Sadly, yes! Only by knowing the old shed layout can the position be judged, but the 1998 view holds little of interest for the railway aficionado. *Terry Gough/MJS*

An earlier view of shed life at Wadebridge, when North Cornwall services were more likely to be hauled by venerable 'T9s'. In January 1952 Nos 30717 and 30729 stand by the shed's 50-foot turntable, proudly displaying their appropriate route discs. This length of the turntable was only sufficient for more modest locos, and Bulleid 'Pacifics' had to turn at Padstow. The siting of the shed was completed around 1895, when the original B&WR facilities on the other side of the line and slightly further west were closed. Note the full bicycle rack and the fully manual nature of the turntable, both signs of the past. Both locos vied with Class 'Ns' on the route right up to their end, which came in August and April 1961 respectively.

Whether by design or accident, the 'turntable' feature at the entrance to Jubilee Field closely represents its forebear at close to the original position. *Maurice Dart collection/MJS*

30586
30586
604
SOUTHERN RAILWAY

Acting as station pilot for the day, 'unique' No 30586 shunts a wide variety of stock in Platform 1 on 10 May 1958. Included in the consist are a 16-ton mineral wagon, a produce van, a livestock vehicle and two Maunsell coaches. With the shunter's pole resting against the furthest van, this must be a quiet time for the station! Note the array of wooden barrows, all clearly stamped 'Wadebridge' – obviously a sign of much shifting of baggage, etc – and the Southern Railway still being proclaimed on the poster boards, ten years after it ceased to exist!

The station canopy and Town Hall clock tower are obvious points of reference. The building between the old goods shed and the station proper, behind the footbridge, has been demolished, leaving the station offices standing alone. These have now been renovated and converted into the Betjeman Centre, a mixture of old people's home and visitor centre. The canopy does not look as attractive in black, but at least it survives. In the right distance, the clock tower remains prominent, but a closer inspection reveals design alterations to the portion visible here, smoothing its lines but in no way enhancing its aesthetic appeal. *Brian Morrison/MJS*

Four views of 'progress'. In early years of this century, around 1913, a porter hauls a laden trolley along platform 1 as steam railmotor No 10 heads off towards the crossover just ahead of it, from whence it will run back into the station to form a return trip to Bodmin North. An open lattice-work LSWR wooden footbridge joins platforms 1 and 2, while the building on the latter is bedecked with a plethora of hoardings. The bridge was replaced by a more utilitarian, concrete structure by the Southern Railway in the mid-1920s.

In the same view on Whit Monday, 18 May 1959, No 30711 appears to be running 'wrong road', but is removing the front two coaches of the 12.58pm Padstow-Waterloo, having worked the service from Padstow (wearing the appropriate express headcode). These two coaches will be used on the Bodmin North service, while the main train will be taken onwards by No 31809. Not as lucky as some of its sisters, No 30711 had only four months to live, despite its healthy appearance, being withdrawn in September 1959. An ex-GWR coach sits in platform 3 on a train to Bodmin Road, while the ventilation shafts on the shed roof have seen amendment over the years.

The date of the third view is 10 September 1980 and desolation and redevelopment are evident – and the weather seems to be commenting on the loss of the railway. The line to Wadebridge Quay, situated behind the distant buildings and accessed by way of the level crossing, closed on 2 April 1973, with all traffic finally disappearing from the station from 4 September 1978. Thankfully, the predilection for car parks and supermarkets on railway land has not occurred here in untimely haste, leaving the site long enough for more enlightened considerations to be taken into account.

The renovated canopy is again seen in the 'present' photograph, and the roadside curb virtually echoes the platform edge, but the 1980s housing redevelopment has obliterated the rest of the previous views. *Lens of Sutton/Michael Mensing/Graham Roose/MJS*

Views of operations at Wadebridge in the early years of this century are not so easy to come by, so this view of LSWR No 639, on a sunny 7 December 1918, is especially welcome. Standing in the goods yard to the west of the shed, the 0-4-2 is in remarkable external condition, with livery and double lining shining brightly as driver and fireman pay their respective attentions, preparing the loco for its next turn of duty. The headcode appears to be Waterloo-Plymouth, and it would be interesting to learn of the working that brought it to this neck of the woods. The LSWR sign, gas lamp, multiplicity of telegraph wires and church in the background all add to the charm of the view.

The church remains, as do the trees on the hillside, but the charm has gone! Once more, by 1998 all trace of the railway has been obliterated. *Peter Treloar collection/MJS*

This delightful shot incorporates the two main influences at Wadebridge – SR and GWR. No 30715 waits in the afternoon sunshine of 22 September 1959 to haul a returning school train to Padstow, while No 5572 runs round, having brought its train from Bodmin Road. Note the chain preventing the driver from falling from the cab, the engine's '3P' power classification above the number, and the large vertical wheel to control the flow on the water column.

The distant houses are all that now link the two views, with the access road to the new estate, appropriately named 'Southern Way', assuming the space of the old trackbed. The distant roofline is common to both views. *Peter Treloar/MJS*

The Town Hall clock tower is again visible here, as Class 'N' No 31834 brings in a very short freight from Padstow on 1 July 1961, past a LSWR lattice-post lower-quadrant signal, unusually tall for such a location but presumably to assist drivers approaching the platform end, whose vision may have been hampered by the station canopy, as all trains stopped here. To the right, No 30586 stands by for more shunting.

The redesigned clock tower roof is more obvious from this angle, and is one of the few common landmarks between the two shots. In the foreground is the car park seen on page 73. *Terry Gough/MJS*

In LSWR days, what appears to be 'T9' No 289 waits for its driver to regain the footplate before setting off for Padstow. The foot of the signal post seen opposite is on the right, while a lower, concrete version sits on the up platform. Note that the poster board, on the wooden W. H. Smith bookstall to the right of the approaching porter, proudly advertises the GWR.

While not exactly in the previous photographer's footsteps, the second picture is nevertheless an interesting view of the scene in the town's railway twilight period. This is the Lea Valley Railway Club's tour to the station in April 1977, comprising a six-car DMU rake, with Bristol-based B802 three-car set leading. Demolition of platform 2's canopy (left) had been achieved by 1970, and on the far left the shed area is now returning to a green field.

Another view of Southern Way and the Betjeman Centre For The Retired, occupying the old station buildings. I wonder if the lady appreciates the significance of where she is sitting! *Lens of Sutton/Graham Roose/MJS*

With the station signboard on platform 2 visible over the railings, there is no mistaking the location. In what appears to be the early part of this century, the approach road and station platforms at Wadebridge have a quietly relaxed air in the late morning sunshine, as two porters lean nonchalantly against the hoardings in the shade. Behind them are all manner of notices and advertisements, while on the railings we are encouraged to sample, among others, the delights of Epps's Coffee, Sunny Island Tea, Camp Coffee, and the *Western Morning News*. With two other signs extolling the virtues of wines, the good people of Wadebridge were obviously thought to be thirsty souls! Cart tracks lead past the gas lamp and buffer stop towards the sign on the right-hand building, which points to the Goods Office.

Major landscaping has occurred in recent years, obliterating much of previous railway infrastructure, but this is the same vantage point, with the single chimney on the former goods shed providing the distinctive point of reference. *Roger Carpenter collection/MJS*

'T9' No 30709 points westward at the station, waiting to start the 1.15pm train to Padstow on 30 June 1960, with leading Bulleid coach S5872S in tow. The Town Hall clock tower is again seen, while to the right of the loco are the surviving buildings of the original Bodmin & Wadebridge Railway, including the railway's original engine shed to the extreme right, just managing to stand upright! Having stood for 126 years at the time of this view, they succumbed just two years later. Note that the ex-LSWR notices, warning against crossing the line other than by the bridge, have been duly amended to serve the SR.

Ancient and more modern railway history have all been swept away, with the ubiquitous motor vehicle again the victor in 1998. *David Holmes/MJS*

Both No 30709 and some of those ancient buildings are seen again, but this time with the train running in the opposite direction. The date is 1954, and the train is Diagram 547, ie for Exeter.

Once more there is nothing to show that a railway ever existed here. In 1998 car parking spaces for a supermarket and other shops now occupy the old trackbed. *Peter Treloar/MJS*

As the railway left Wadebridge it crossed Molesworth Street, at the time of this view the main A39 road through the town. On the beautifully sunny afternoon of 22 September 1959, the unadvertised 4.25pm returning school train leaves Wadebridge bound for Padstow. In a superbly evocative scene from the period, a helmeted policeman holds back the traffic as No 30715 crosses the road behind the safety of the gates, and two schoolgirls, presumably from the train, also wait to cross the railway. The locomotive was a long-time stalwart of the area, completing over 2 million miles by the time of her withdrawal. Signs proclaim the way to the Free Car Park and advertise D. L. Lang's Fish & Chips Snack Bar, but the significance of the '456' sign is a mystery!

By 1998 the A39 trunk road has been diverted around the northern outskirts of the town, but the now minor road through the town is still extremely busy, in view of the general increase in road traffic and the requirement of many to access the town's shops. Additionally the road to the left has been doubled in width, utilising the old trackbed. The fish cafe has metamorphosed into a restaurant and take-away, with such delights as 'Steak & Chips £4.50' available as well as simpler fare. The main corner period building has seen both renovation and some alteration: chimneys have gone, as has some beading on the side wall, but overall the facade has a much smarter feel, with attractive street lamps added. *Peter Treloar/MJS*

On to Padstow

Above For the whole of the 6 miles or so from Wadebridge to Padstow the railway hugged the shoreline of the River Camel, giving supremely attractive views from the virtually level track. For those arriving on holiday by train, anticipating, perhaps, their beach days in Padstow, the sight of the water and the increasing amounts of sand, especially at low tide, as the journey approached its end added to the excitement and anticipation. The scenery and surrounding countryside is beautifully depicted in this view of the train that probably brought more to the coast for holidays than any other – the 'Atlantic Coast Express'. On 1 July 1961 'Battle of Britain' 'Pacific' No 34110 *66 Squadron*, last of the Class, heads past Oldtown Cove, only a mile or so out from Padstow, with, unusually, five through coaches from the much longer train that had left Waterloo. It was far more normal for the train to only have two coaches left at this stage of its journey, others having been 'dropped off' for destinations in Devon and Cornwall. Note that the loco is devoid of nameplates, including the Squadron's crest, a fate that befell so many in their latter days. The loco was withdrawn from Exmouth Junction (72A) in November 1963 and the last 'ACE' ran on 4 September 1964. *Terry Gough*

Opposite page This very slightly lower angle from the same vantage point on the same day provides a view of the other type of passenger train that ran this route, the service from Bodmin to Padstow. No 4666 of Wadebridge shed hurries along with Maunsell coach set 27 forming the 4.05pm Bodmin North-Padstow train. Note that although it is an ex-GWR loco, it is correctly wearing the SR single disc code for the journey.

Thankfully, due to far-sighted Council thinking, this stretch can still be enjoyed by thousands, either by walking or cycling the Camel Trail. A seat has thoughtfully been provided here to enjoy the views of the cove and the river, and two walkers enjoy a rest in the warm sunshine of 22 May 1998. *Terry Gough/MJS*

Padstow, River Camel.

Running towards Padstow, the railway rounds the headland (seen in the middle distance) from Oldtown Cove and runs on to the bridge spanning Little Petherick Creek. On an unknown date, a tank locomotive has hauled three coaches bound for Bodmin over the impressive three-span, two-pier bridge, watched from Dennis Hill by a resting walker. The tank is working up the 1 in 132 gradient around the 20-chain-radius curve, and, having left the three 130-foot spans, completes the crossing of the creek on the low embankment, built for the railway in 1899. The fields in the distance look well farmed but a little sparse from this angle.

In 1998 it is virtually impossible to replicate the view from Dennis Hill exactly, due to rampant growth of bushes and trees. The bridge, however, still stands to give passage to walkers and cyclists on the Camel Trail. Its width is restricted for the latter, but even in steam days there cannot have been much spare space on either side of a train. *Peter Treloar collection/MJS*

The approach to the town, 260 miles from Waterloo, saw buildings gradually increase on the railway's left, gradually being elevated ever higher above the tracks as the railway continued to hug the coast. The final swing into the terminus saw trains pass the 'new' turntable, and this can just be seen above the cab roof of No 31904 as it gathers speed away from the terminus on 1 July 1961 with the 3.13pm to Okehampton. Built in 1947 and measuring 70 feet in diameter to accommodate larger engines, the turntable took over from the one built in 1910, which in turn had replaced the original when the land was needed for construction of South Jetty and its two sidings. It was unusual for a 'U1' Class loco to reach Padstow, Class 'Ns' being more normal motive power, but No 31904 and a small handful of its sisters spent the summer of 1961 'on trial' in the area. As they resumed duties from their more usual homes of Stewart's Lane and Tonbridge sheds at the end of the summer and did not return, one can only assume that the experiment was not a success. In the background, to the left, Class 'N' No 31837 waits to form the 6pm train over the North Cornwall route.

Due to buildings and inaccessibility, the previous high vantage point is again impossible. This, however, is the view from the Camel Trail as it enters Padstow. Hardly recognisable, it is true, but the headland is common to both views and the retaining wall of the old turntable still remains, now without its safety fencing. *Terry Gough/MJS*

The turntable is seen again here on 2 July 1958 as No 30712, still wearing its 'main line' disc headcode, turns itself by means of vacuum, ready to be facing the correct way for its next turn of duty. Across the river the hills around Porthilly can be seen.

The only thing that can be easily turned in 1998 is a motor vehicle! A small industrial unit now resides here, with turning space for the end of a large car park in front of it and the entrance for the Camel Trail coming in from the right. *Terry Gough/MJS*

Swinging slightly to the right of the view opposite, and looking, just a few minutes later, back towards the journey just covered, we see 'West Country' No 34096 *Trevone* gliding easily in towards the terminus with the remaining two coaches of the 'Atlantic Coast Express' on 2 July 1958. The fireman, having temporarily completed his duties, looks over the driver's shoulder – eyeing the photographer?

More light industrial units and car parking spaces now cover the tracks, with the Camel Trail entering between the two 'No Entry' signs, just to the right of the pick-up truck. *Terry Gough/MJS*

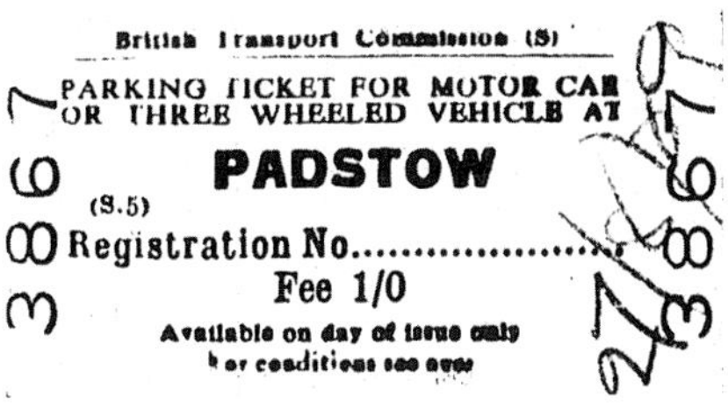

British Transport Commission (S)

PARKING TICKET FOR MOTOR CAR OR THREE WHEELED VEHICLE AT

PADSTOW

(S.5)

Registration No.......................

Fee 1/0

Available on day of issue only

For conditions see over

3867

On 2 July 1958, on the approach to South Jetty, No 30712 has turned and eased from the turntable to take up position to shunt stock to form the 5.06pm to Wadebridge. The driver peers towards the station area, as his charge slowly eases backwards, past a fish-curing shed. Note the somewhat primitive staff accommodation afforded by the grounded coach bodies on the left. An Exmouth Junction (72A) resident for the whole of its British Railways life, until withdrawal in March 1959, No 30712 spent much of this time working in Cornwall.

The old ocean fish terminal buildings on the left, part of the fish-curing shed on the right, and even the gap in the hedge line on the hills in the background, all still remain, but elsewhere everything has changed. A car park for the town now occupies this site; the proximity of the Camel Trail can be judged by the compound of Padstow Cycle Hire. *Terry Gough/MJS*

Turning through 90 degrees, the 1899 terminus can now be seen, complete with attendant signal box and sidings. No 30709, another long-term servant of the route, waits in the single platform with the 3.13pm train to Exeter on a dull 19 August 1958. The squat signal box, lattice-post signal and wooden lamp room on the platform all make for a delightful view of past operation. The signal box closed on 9 January 1966.

London and South Western Ry.

787

FROM WATERLOO TO

PADSTOW

The station building, The Metropole Hotel behind, the houses on the bank on the left, and the old fish sheds on the right all confirm the location, which now sees many more wheels than in previous times! *E. Wilmhurst/MJS*

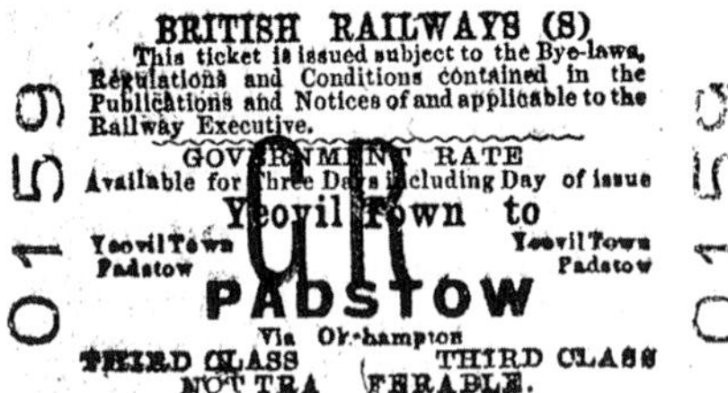
BRITISH RAILWAYS (S)
This ticket is issued subject to the Bye-laws, Regulations and Conditions contained in the Publications and Notices of and applicable to the Railway Executive.
GOVERNMENT RATE
Available for Three Days including Day of issue
Yeovil Town to
Yeovil Town Padstow
Yeovil Town Padstow
PADSTOW
Via Okehampton
THIRD CLASS THIRD CLASS
NOT TRANSFERABLE.
0159 0159

The attractive signal box and post are again seen on the left in this 15 July 1960 photograph. Two years on from the previous view, the stock of the 3.13pm to Exeter is again seen, as No 30719 shunts Maunsell set 236 in the station sidings, before finally moving into the platform. Evidence of some hard work is seen on the loco's smokebox.

Twelve months later, on 1 July 1961, we see No 31904 being oiled prior to working the 3.13, while more normal motive power, No 31837, heads more modern stock that is being prepared for the 6pm following service along the North Cornwall line. Note that the grounded coach bodies, relics of the rapid expansion of the railway here in the early years of this century, have now gone.

The station building still stands on the left, previously hidden by the signal box, and the old fish shed still finds employment, but otherwise there is much less to interest the railway enthusiast! *R. C. Riley/Terry Gough/MJS*

A very smartly turned out No 30203 has plenty of steam in hand as it waits to form the 5.06pm departure for Wadebridge on 17 April 1954, made up of four coaches rather than the more usual two. Although the surface of the platform could perhaps do with some renovation, the area has been kept clean and tidy, as has the stock. The presence of the brake-van on the right shows that not only passenger traffic is still being handled. Like so many of the engines operating in the area, No 30203 spent many years at Wadebridge shed, including the whole of its British Railways life, before being withdrawn in January 1956. Less than an hour later the 'Atlantic Coast Express' will arrive behind No 34058 *Sir Frederick Pile*.

In 1998, as seen before, the fish sheds still remain, as do the platform and station buildings, the latter in use as offices for Customs & Excise and the local Town Council; the solid nature of the buildings is in keeping with others on the LSWR's North Cornwall line. The ubiquitous car has taken over the space between, and coaches regularly ply their customers to a point at the far end, as seen here. The roofs of the main part of the town can just be see to the right of the Metropole Hotel. *B. K. B. Green, Maurice Dart collection/MJS*

1745 British Transport Commission (S)
PADSTOW
PLATFORM TICKET 2d.
Available one hour on day of issue only.
Not valid in trains. Not transferable.
To be given up when leaving platform.
For conditions see over 1745

Seen from the elevated road leading down to the station, No 31845 has arrived at the terminus with the 5.51pm from Okehampton, formed of Maunsell set 172, on 1 July 1961. Most of the passengers have already disembarked and are leaving the station, but one is only just opening his carriage door – perhaps he enjoyed a pleasant sleep for the final part of the journey! Being now well into the evening, the carriage sidings are occupied by stock ready for the next day's services. Note the slightly unusual sign and almost complete lack of cars – an apparently permanent enough scene, but steam ceased on the route from 1964 and the line from Wadebridge closed completely on 30 January 1967.

The advertising hoarding and telegraph pole on the right have gone, as has the station canopy, small approach road building and some chimneys. The fencing looks as though it might be the original, but the far end has seen remodelling. Double yellow lines now forbid parking on the station side, a reversal of previous practice. In 1998 it was mooted that the former fish sheds across the car park should be swept away and their occupants transferred to new buildings on the platform site; consequently, this 'present' view could soon be dramatically changed! *Terry Gough/MJS*

To most visitors to Padstow by rail, operations ceased at the buffer stops in the platform, but since earliest times there had been sidings extending past these, reaching further towards the main town along the dockside. In the early years of this century No 465 prepares to haul a rake of empty LSWR wagons eastwards away from the town, perhaps connected with the burgeoning fish trade. Although on freight duty, the external condition of the engine confirms the advantage of having locomotives allocated to individual crews, a pre-Grouping practice for this class in the area.

The dock sidings saw considerable traffic for over 50 years, even including china clay for a period, but dramatically declined after the mid-1950s, with freight traffic withdrawn from the town from 7 September 1964. The trackwork here was taken up before the final end of services in 1967 and, once again, the influence of the motor vehicle has since been felt and the whole of the former trackbed along the docks is now given over to car parking. This is the view in May 1998. *Peter Treloar collection/MJS*

Those buffer stops and the freight sidings can again be seen in this 15 September 1958 view from the road embankment opposite the end of the platform. A 'T9' has just run round its train, formed of what appears to be set 169, while a six-coach rake, with a representative of set 833 at this end, stands in the middle road. The compact but eminently functional layout of the terminus is well judged from this view, but the buses parked on the sloping approach road on the extreme right could have desired a better waiting area!

The sweeping road is common to both views, this lower angle dictated by the inaccessibility of the previous embankment spot. Seen early in the morning of a summer Friday, the space to the left will very shortly be filled with incoming coaches, parking here rather than on the approach road. *A. P. Grierson, Stephenson Locomotive Society, Maurice Dart collection/MJS*

Above **Finally, two views from happier times. The first is a scene from early in the railway's history, probably within a year or two of the line's opening in 1899, judging by the clean nature of the area, showing the original track layout. In subsequent years will be added sidings behind the rail-linked fish shed in the centre, a third platform track for carriage storage, warehousing, and a water tank, and even the removal of the turntable to the final position slightly further away from the station. At this time, the Metropole Hotel, opened in 1900, traded under its original name of the South Western hotel, advertising Ladies' Drawing Rooms among other facilities!** *Lens of Sutton*

Below **This delightful view is full of atmosphere and railway interest, despite being late in the line's history. In another photograph taken on 1 July 1961, No 31837 shunts stock prior to moving it into the platform to form a service to Exeter. Much of the final layout, superbly encapsulated in this elevated view, including the rarely photographed goods shed on the platform side, makes an intriguing comparison with the shot above.** *Terry Gough*

74 1st JUNE to 30th SEPTEMBER, 1909, or until further notice.

BODMIN AND WADEBRIDGE BRANCH.

FOR SPEED RESTRICTIONS SEE PAGES A, B, C & D.

This is a Single Line and is worked under the Regulations for working Single Lines by the Electric Train Tablet Block System.

London and South Western Trains between Wadebridge, Boscarne Junction, and Bodmin, S.W., and Great Western Trains between Wadebridge, Boscarne Junction, and Bodmin, G.W., and *vice versa.*

L. & S. W. Up and Down Passenger Trains and Cars will call when required at the Shooting Range Platform (situated about 1¼ miles from Wadebridge) to set down or take up not less than 6 Volunteers proceeding from or to Bodmin. Bodmin to arrange.

Wenford Branch.—Only one Engine in Steam is allowed on this Branch at one time. The speed of Trains must be so controlled that they may be stopped immediately in case of emergency.

GROGLEY HALT.—Lamps are not provided at Grogley Halt, and the Cars shown to call there will only do so during daylight.

DOWN LONDON AND SOUTH WESTERN AND UP GREAT WESTERN TRAINS.—WEEK DAYS ONLY.

m. c.	STATIONS AND HALTS.	1		2		3		4		5		6		7		8		9		10		11		12		13	
		S.W. Car.		S.W. Car.		G.W. Pass.		S.W. Mixed.		S.W. Car.		G.W. Pass.		*S.W. Mineral when required.*		S.W. Car.		G.W. Pass.		*S.W. Mineral when required.*		S.W. Car.		S.W. Car.		G.W. Pass.	
		arr.	dep.	arr.	dep.	arr.	dep.	arr.	dep.	arr.	dep.	arr.	dep.	arr.	dep.	arr.	dep.	arr.	dep.	arr.	dep.	arr.	dep.	arr.	dep.	arr.	dep.
		a.m.	a.m.	a.m.	a.m.	a.m.	a.m.	a.m.	a.m.	a.m.	a.m.	a.m.	a.m.	a.m.	a.m.	a.m.	a.m.	a.m.	a.m.	a.m.	a.m.	p.m.	p.m.	p.m.	p.m.	p.m.	p.m.
...	**Wadebridge**	...	6 15	...	7 5	...	7 48	...	8 43	...	9 34	...	9 48		*9 58*	...	1027	...	1138		*11 48*	...	1216	...	1 5	A	1 45
2 72	Grogley Halt	6 21½	6 22	7 11½	7 12	...	...	...	...	9 40½	9 41	...	...	...	...	1033½	10 34	...	...	...	...	1222½	1223	1 11½	1 12	...	—
4 31	Nanstallon Halt	6 26	6 26½	7 16	7 16½	...	...	...	...	9 45	9 45½	...	...	...	...	10 38	1038½	...	...	...	...	1227	1227½	1 16	1 16½	...	—
4 61	Boscarne Junction	6 27½	6 28	7 17½	7 18	7 57	7 58	8 54	8 55	9 46½	9 47	9 57	9 58	*10 11*	...	1039½	10 40	11 47	11 48	*12 15*	...	1228½	1229	1 17½	1 18	1 55	1 56
...	**Bodmin, G.W.**	...	...	...	...	8 8	...	...	...	...	...	10 8	...			...	...	1158	...			...	...	...	...	2 8	...
5 19	Dunmere Halt	6 29½	6 30	7 19½	7 20			...	...	9 48½	9 49	...	...	...	...	1041½	10 42			...	...	1230½	1231	1 19½	1 20		
6 50	**Bodmin, L. & S.W.**	6 34	...	7 24	...	...	...	9 0	...	9 53	...	...	...	...	...	10 46	...	...	...	...	...	1235	...	1 24	...	...	—

STATIONS AND HALTS.	14		15		16		17		18		19		20		21		22		23		24		25		26	
	S.W. Con. Gds.		*S.W. Goods. Not Sats.*		*S.W. Mixed. Sats. only.*		*G.W. Con. Gds.*		*G.W. Goods. When required.*		G.W. Pass.		S.W. Car.		S.W. Car.		S.W. Car.		G.W. Mixed.		G.W. Pass.		S.W. Car.		*G.W. Pass. Sats. F.*	
	arr	dep.	arr.	dep.	arr.	dep.	arr.	dep.	arr.	dep.	arr.	dep.	arr.	dep.	arr.	dep.	arr.	dep.	arr.	dep.	arr.	dep.	arr.	dep.	arr.	dep.
	p.m	p.m.	p.m.	p.m.	p.m.	p.m.	p.m.	p.m.	p.m.	p.m.	p.m.	p.m.	p.m.	p.m.	p.m.	p.m.	p.m.	p.m.	p.m.	p.m.	p.m.	p.m.	p.m.	p.m.	p.m.	p.m.
Wadebridge	E	*1 57*	...	*2 37*	...	*2 37*	E	*2 48*	...	...	...	3 43	...	4 10	...	4 54	...	6 2	...	6 17	...	8 21	...	8 32	...	*10 20*
Grogley Halt	...	...	...	...	...	...	...	...	...	...	...	...	4 16½	4 17	5 0½	5 1	6 8½	6 9	...	...	...	...	8 38½	8 39	...	—
Nanstallon Halt	...	...	...	...	...	...	...	...	...	...	...	...	4 21	4 21½	5 5	5 5½	6 13	6 13½	...	...	...	...	8 43	8 43½	...	...
Boscarne Junction	*2 9*	...	*2 49*	*2 53*	*2 48*	*2 49*	...	*3 0*	...	*3 29*	3 52	3 53	4 22½	4 23	5 6½	5 7	6 14½	6 15	6 27	6 28	8 30	8 31	8 44½	8 45	*10 29*	*10 30*
Bodmin, G.W.			...	...	...	...	*3 7*	...	*3 39*	...	4 3	...	...	...	...	...	...	...	6 40	...	8 41	...	...	...	*10 40*	...
Dunmere Halt	...	...	...	...	...	...							4 24½	4 25	5 8½	5 9	6 16½	6 17					8 46½	8 47		
Bodmin, L. & S. W.	...	...	*2 59*	...	*2 54*	...	...	...	...	...	...	...	4 29	...	5 13	...	6 21	...	...	...	...	...	8 51	...	...	—

UP LONDON AND SOUTH WESTERN AND DOWN GREAT WESTERN TRAINS.—WEEK DAYS ONLY.

m. c.	STATIONS AND HALTS.	1		2		3		4		5		6		7		8		9		10		11		12		13	
		S.W. Car.		G.W. Pass.		S.W. Car.		S.W. Pass. C		G.W. Pass.		S.W. Car.		S.W. Car.		G.W. Pass.		S.W. Car.				G.W. Pass.		*G.W. Con. Gds.*		S.W. Car.	
		arr.	dep.	arr.	dep.	arr.	dep.	arr.	dep.	arr.	dep.	arr.	dep.	arr.	dep.	arr.	dep.	arr.	dep.	arr.	dep.	arr.	dep.	arr.	dep.	arr.	dep.
		a.m.	a.m.	a.m.	a.m.	a.m.	a.m.	a.m.	a.m.	a.m.	a.m.	a.m.	a.m.	a.m.	a.m.	a.m.	a.m.	p.m.	p.m.			p.m.	p.m.	p.m.	p.m.	p.m.	p.m.
...	**Bodmin, L. & S.W.**	...	6 43	...	...	...	8 19	...	9 8	...	...	...	10 7	...	1050	...	...	...	1240	...	...	...	...	...	...	...	2 19
1 31	Dunmere Halt	6 46½	6 47	...	...	8 22½	8 23	C	...	...	...	1010½	10 11	1053½	10 54	...	...	1243½	1244	...	...	...	...	...	...	2 22½	2 23
...	**Bodmin, G.W.**	...	...	A	7 12	...	...	...	...	...	9 17	...	...	...	...	...	11 13	...	...	...	...	A	1 12	E	*1 42*	...	...
1 69	Boscarne Junction	6 48	6 48½	7 19	7 20	8 24	8 24½	9 11	9 12	9 22	9 23	10 12	1012½	10 55	1055½	11 18	11 19	1245	1245½	...	...	1 19	1 20	*1 47*	*2 0*	2 24	2 24½
2 19	Nanstallon Halt	6 49½	6 50	...	...	8 25½	8 26	C	...	...	...	1013½	10 14	1056½	10 57	...	...	1246½	12 47	...	...	...	...	...	...	2 25½	2 26
3 58	Grogley Halt	6 53	6 53½	...	...	8 29	8 29½	C	...	...	...	10 17	1017½	11 0	11 0½	...	...	12 50	1250½	...	...	...	...	...	...	2 29	2 29½
6 50	**Wadebridge**	7 0	...	7 31	...	8 36	...	9 21	...	9 33	...	1024	...	11 7	...	11 29	...	1257	...	...	...	1 31	...	*2 12*	...	2 36	—

STATIONS AND HALTS.	14		15		16		17		18		19		20		21		22		23		24		25		26	
	S.W. Con. Gds.		G.W. Pass.		*G.W. Goods. When required*		*S.W. Mineral when required.*		S.W. Goods.		*S.W. Mineral when required.*		S.W. Car.		G.W. Pass.		S.W Car.		S.W. Car.		G.W. Pass.		S.W. Car.		*G.W. Pass. Sats. F.*	
	arr.	dep.	arr.	dep.	arr.	dep.	arr.	dep.	arr.	dep.	arr.	dep.	arr.	dep.	arr.	dep.	arr.	dep.	arr.	dep.	arr.	dep.	arr.	dep.	arr.	dep.
	p.m.	p.m.	p.m.	p.m.	p.m.	p.m.	p.m.	p.m.	p.m.	p.m.	p.m.	p.m.	p.m	p.m.	p.m.	p.m.	p.m.	p.m.	p.m.	p.m.	p.m.	p.m.	p.m.	p.m.	p.m.	p.m.
Bodmin, L. & S.W.	...	...	...	...	...	...	...	...	...	3 50	...	...	...	4 33	...	...	...	5 35	...	7 44	...	...	...	9 10	...	—
Dunmere Halt	...	...	...	...	...	...	...	...	...	...	...	...	4 36½	4 37	...	...	5 38½	5 39	7 47½	7 48	...	...	9 13½	9 14	...	—
Bodmin, G.W.	...	...	...	3 8	...	*3 15*	...	...	...	...	...	...	...	...	B	5 17	...	...	...	...	...	7 56	...	...	...	*9 57*
Boscarne Junction	E	*3 0*	3 13	3 14	*3 21*	...	...	*3 25*	3 55	3 57	...	*4 27*	4 38	4 38½	5 22	5 23	5 40	5 40½	7 49	7 49½	8 1	8 2	9 15	9 15½	*10 2*	*10 3*
Nanstallon Halt	...	...	...	...			...	...	...	...	...	...	4 39½	4 40	...	...	5 41½	5 42	7 50½	7 51	...	...	9 16½	9 17	...	—
Grogley Halt	...	...	...	...			...	...	...	...	...	...	4 43	4 43½	...	...	5 45	5 45½	7 54	7 54½	...	...	9 20	9 20½	...	—
Wadebridge	*3 12*	...	3 24	...	...	...	*3 42*	...	4 9	...	*4 37*	...	4 50	...	5 33	...	5 52	...	8 1	...	8 12	...	9 27	...	*10 13*	—

A Mixed Trains. B Runs 4 minutes later during July, August and September. C Calls at Dunmere, Nanstallon and Grogley Halts on the second Tuesday in each month. E Nos. 14 Down and 14 Up will run when required and as ordered by Wadebridge. They will not run when Nos. 17 Down and 12 Up run. F July, August and September only.

A Mineral Train, as required, will run on Week-days, as under:—

Dist. from Wadebrdge m. c.		1 arr. a.m.	1 dep. a.m.	2 arr. a.m.	2 dep. a.m.
—	Wadebridge	...	9 58	...	11 48
2 69	Grogley Halt	...	...	11 54	11 56
4 01	Ruthern Bridge	...	...	12 0	12 4
—	Grogley Halt	...	...	12 8	12 10
4 61	Boscarne Junction	10 11	10 30	12 15	12 55
5 66	Dunmere Junction	10 35	11 4	1 0	1 15
8 14	Helland	11 24	11 29	1 33	1 38
10 26	Tresarrett	11 39	11 49	1 48	1 56
11 24	Clay Co.'s Siding	11 55	12 5	2 2	2 12
11 64	Wenford	12 10	...	2 17	...

Dist. from Wenford. m. c.		1 arr. p.m.	1 dep. p.m.	2 arr. p.m.	2 dep. p.m.
—	Wenford	...	1 45	...	2 50
0 40	Clay Co.'s Siding	1 50	2 0	2 55	3 5
1 38	Tresarrett	2 6	2 16	3 11	3 16
3 50	Helland	2 25	2 28	3 25	3 28
6 58	Dunmere Junction	2 49	3 0	3 48	4 5
7 3	Boscarne Junction	3 5	3 25	4 9	4 27
7 41	Nanstallon	3 28	3 32	...	—
11 64	Wadebridge	3 42	...	4 37	—

When No. 1 runs No. 2 will not run, and when No. 2 runs No. 1 will not run. Wadebridge to arrange.

LSWR/GWR, Summer 1909

Table 49

Table 49 BODMIN, WADEBRIDGE and PADSTOW

Second class only

WEEKDAYS ONLY

Miles from Bodmin N.	Miles			Mondays to Fridays																				
				am	am	am	am	am	am	am	am	am	am		pm	pm	pm	pm	pm		pm	pm	pm	pm
		Bodmin Road	dep	6 50	..	7 50	..	..	8 40	..	1010	..	1125	..	..	1225	1 35	..	..	..	2 20	..	..	4 35
		Bodmin General	arr	7 0	..	7 58	..	..	8 48	..	1025	..	1133	..	..	1233	1 43	..	..	..	2 28	..	..	4 43
	3½	Bodmin General	dep	..	7 27	8 3	..	..	..	8 58	1040	..	..	..	..	1238	..	..	..	..	2 38	..	..	4 50
	—	Bodmin North	dep	..	..	..	..	8 45	..	..	..	1110	..	..	..	..	..	..	2 0	..	..	4 23	..	..
1½	—	Dunmere Halt		..	..	..	..	8 48	..	..	..	1114	..	..	..	..	..	..	2 4	..	..	4 27	..	..
2¼	6½	Nanstallon Halt		..	7 34	8 15	..	8 51	..	..	..	1117	..	..	..	1245	..	..	2 7	..	..	4 30	..	4 57
3¾	8	Grogley Halt		..	7 39	..	..	8 56	..	..	..	1121	..	..	..	..	..	..	2 11	..	..	4 34	..	..
6¾	11	Wadebridge	arr	..	7 48	8 27	..	9 6	..	9 16	1052	1129	..	..	..	1257	..	..	2 19	..	2 55	4 42	..	5 9
		Wadebridge	dep	..	7 50	8 30	9 5	..	..	..	11 0	1131	..	..	12 5	..	..	1 15	2 24	..	..	..	4 50	5 10
12¼	16½	Padstow	arr	..	8 0	8 40	9 14	..	..	..	1110	1140	..	..	1215	..	..	1 29	2 34	..	..	..	5 0	5 21

		Mondays to Fridays—continued									Saturdays													
		pm	pm		pm		pm		pm		am	am	am		am	am	am	am		am	am	am		am
Bodmin Road	dep	..	..	..	6 5	..	6 55	..	7 55	..	6 50	..	..	..	7 50	..	..	8 45	..	9 15	10 2	1030	..	..
Bodmin General	arr	..	..	..	6 13	..	7 3	..	8 3	..	7 0	..	..	..	7 58	..	..	8 54	..	9 23	1011	1038	..	..
Bodmin General	dep	..	..	..	6 18	..	..	..	8 10	..	..	..	7 27	..	8 8	..	..	9 0	..	..	1015	..	..	..
Bodmin North	dep	5 44	..	..	..	..	..	..	..	..	..	..	..	..	..	8 44	..	..	..	..	..	..	..	1110
Dunmere Halt		5 48	..	..	..	..	..	..	..	..	..	..	..	..	..	8 48	..	..	..	..	..	..	..	1113
Nanstallon Halt		5 51	..	..	6 27	..	..	..	8 17	..	..	..	7 34	..	8 15	8 51	..	9 8	..	..	..	..	..	1116
Grogley Halt		5 55	..	..	6 32	..	..	..	8 22	..	..	..	7 39	..	..	8 54	..	..	..	..	..	..	..	1121
Wadebridge	arr	6 3	..	..	6 42	..	..	..	8 30	..	..	..	7 48	..	8 27	9 4	..	9 18	..	..	1033	..	..	1130
Wadebridge	dep	..	6 30	..	..	..	..	..	8 32	..	..	7 16	7 50	..	8 40	..	9 10	9 20	..	..	1034	..	..	1140
Padstow	arr	..	6 40	..	..	..	..	..	8 42	..	..	7 26	8 0	..	8 50	..	9 19	9 29	..	..	1043	..	..	1149

		Saturdays—continued																						
		pm	pm		pm	pm		pm	pm	pm	pm	pm	pm		pm	pm	pm	pm		pm	pm		pm	pm
Bodmin Road	dep	..	12 5	..	..	1 52	..	..	2 20	3 15	..	4 20	..	..	5 10	..	..	6 22	..	7 0	8 25	..	9 0	1015
Bodmin General	arr	..	1213	..	..	2 0	..	..	2 28	3 25	..	4 28	..	..	5 18	..	..	6 31	..	7 8	8 33	..	9 8	1023
Bodmin General	dep	..	1218	..	..	..	..	..	2 33	..	..	..	..	..	5 22	..	..	6 40	..	..	8 38	..	..	..
Bodmin North	dep	..	..	..	..	..	..	2 0	..	..	4 5	..	..	..	..	..	..	..	..	..	..	..	..	..
Dunmere Halt		..	..	..	..	..	..	2 4	..	..	4 9	..	..	..	..	..	..	..	..	..	..	..	..	..
Nanstallon Halt		..	1226	..	..	..	..	2 7	..	..	4 12	..	..	..	5 31	..	..	6 49	..	..	8 45	..	..	..
Grogley Halt		..	..	..	..	..	..	2 11	..	..	4 16	..	..	..	..	..	..	6 54	..	..	8 50	..	..	..
Wadebridge	arr	..	1238	..	..	..	..	2 19	2 51	..	4 24	..	..	..	5 43	..	..	7 2	..	..	8 58	..	..	..
Wadebridge	dep	1220	..	..	1 15	..	..	2 24	..	..	4 25	..	4 50	..	..	5 48	6 30	7 3	..	..	9 0	..	..	..
Padstow	arr	1230	..	..	1 30	..	..	2 34	..	..	4 35	..	5 0	..	..	6 0	6 40	7 12	..	..	9 10	..	..	..

Miles	Miles			Mondays to Fridays																				
				am	am	am	am	am	am	am	am	am	am	am		am	pm	pm	pm	pm	pm	pm		pm
		Padstow	dep	..	..	..	..	8 12	8 48	..	9 5	9 33	..	1120	..	1155	1 0	..	..	2 52	3 10	..	..	..
5½	5½	Wadebridge	arr	..	..	..	..	8 21	8 57	..	9 14	9 42	..	1129	..	12 4	1 9	..	..	3 1	3 19	..	..	..
		Wadebridge	dep	6 50	..	..	7 58	8 30	..	..	9 17	..	9 50	1132	..	1225	..	..	1 25	3 9	..	3 30	..	5 12
8½	8½	Grogley Halt		6 58	..	..	8 6	8 38	..	..	..	..	9 58	1140	..	1233	..	..	1 33	3 17	..	..	..	5 20
10	10	Nanstallon Halt		7 2	..	..	8 10	8 42	..	..	9 29	..	10 2	1144	..	1237	..	..	1 37	3 21	..	..	..	5 24
10¾	—	Dunmere Halt		..	..	..	8 14	..	..	..	..	..	10 6	..	..	1241	..	..	..	3 25	..	..	..	5 28
12¼	—	Bodmin North	arr	..	..	..	8 18	..	..	..	..	..	1010	..	..	1245	..	..	..	3 29	..	..	..	5 32
—	13	Bodmin General	arr	7 12	..	..	..	8 53	..	..	9 40	..	..	1154	..	..	..	..	1 47	..	..	3 50	..	..
		Bodmin General	dep	..	7 15	8 5	..	..	..	9 20	9 45	..	..	12 8	..	..	..	1 20	1 55	..	..	3 58	..	..
—	16½	Bodmin Road	arr	..	7 22	8 12	..	..	..	9 27	9 52	..	..	1210	..	..	..	1 27	2 2	..	..	4 6	..	..

		Mondays to Fridays—continued											Saturdays											
		pm		pm	pm	pm		pm		pm	pm		am	am	am	am	am	am	am		pm	am		am
Padstow	dep	5 24	..	6 0	6 20	..	..	..	..	9 0	..	..	..	..	..	..	8 12	8 30	9 0	..	..	11 0	..	1115
Wadebridge	arr	5 33	..	6 9	6 29	..	..	..	..	9 9	..	..	..	..	..	..	8 21	8 39	9 9	..	..	11 9	..	1124
Wadebridge	dep	5 34	..	6 10	..	..	..	7 45	..	..	..	..	6 50	..	..	7 58	8 28	..	9 19	..	9 50	..	..	1125
Grogley Halt		..	..	6 18	..	..	..	7 53	..	..	..	..	6 57	..	..	8 5	8 36	..	..	..	9 58	..	..	..
Nanstallon Halt		5 46	..	6 22	..	..	..	7 57	..	..	..	..	7 2	..	..	8 10	8 40	..	9 31	..	10 2	..	..	1137
Dunmere Halt		..	..	..	..	..	..	..	..	..	..	..	..	..	..	8 14	..	..	..	..	10 5	..	..	..
Bodmin North	arr	..	..	..	..	..	..	..	..	..	..	..	..	..	..	8 18	..	..	..	..	1010	..	..	..
Bodmin General	arr	5 58	..	6 33	..	..	..	9 7	..	..	..	..	7 12	..	..	..	8 51	..	9 41	..	..	..	..	1147
Bodmin General	dep	6 3	..	6 38	..	7 33	..	9 16	..	..	1015	..	7 15	7 20	8 13	..	9 3	..	9 45	..	..	..	..	1152
Bodmin Road	arr	6 10	..	6 45	..	7 40	..	9 23	..	..	1022	..	7 22	7 27	8 20	..	9 10	..	9 52	..	..	..	..	12 0

		Saturdays—continued																						
		am	pm	pm	pm	pm	pm	pm	pm		pm	pm	pm	pm		pm		pm	pm		pm	pm	pm	
Padstow	dep	1155	..	1 0	..	..	2 52	3 10	..	..	..	4 40	..	6 0	..	6 20	..	..	7 45	..	..	9 20	..	..
Wadebridge	arr	12 4	..	1 9	..	..	3 1	3 19	..	..	..	4 49	..	6 9	..	6 29	..	..	7 54	..	..	9 29	..	..
Wadebridge	dep	12 5	..	..	..	1 13	3 8	..	3 34	..	..	5 11	..	6 10	..	..	..	..	7 55	..	..	..	..	..
Grogley Halt		1214	..	..	..	1 20	3 16	..	..	..	..	5 19	..	..	..	..	..	..	8 2	..	..	..	..	..
Nanstallon Halt		1218	..	..	..	1 25	3 21	..	..	..	..	5 24	..	..	..	..	..	..	8 7	..	..	..	..	..
Dunmere Halt		1221	..	..	..	..	3 25	..	..	..	..	5 27	..	..	..	..	..	..	..	..	..	..	..	..
Bodmin North	arr	1226	..	..	..	..	3 29	..	..	..	..	5 32	..	..	..	..	..	..	..	..	..	..	..	..
Bodmin General	arr	..	..	..	..	1 35	..	..	3 54	..	..	..	..	6 33	..	..	..	..	8 17	..	..	..	..	..
Bodmin General	dep	..	1240	..	1 15	1 40	..	..	4 0	..	4 35	..	5 40	6 37	..	..	..	7 33	..	..	8 45	..	9 38	..
Bodmin Road	arr	..	1247	..	1 22	1 47	..	..	4 7	..	4 42	..	5 47	6 45	..	..	..	7 40	..	..	8 52	..	9 45	..

On SUNDAYS passengers holding through rail tickets may travel by Southern National Omnibus between Bodmin Road and Wadebridge

BR, Winter 1961/2

Table 97 **BODMIN ROAD, BODMIN, and WADEBRIDGE**

Miles			Week Days only																				
			a.m	a.m		a.m	a.m	a.m		p.m	p.m		p.m	p.m		p.m	p.m		p.m	p.m		p.m	p.m	p.m
			D	E		S		S					S			E	S							
—	Bodmin Road	dep	8 0	8 57	..	9 15	1010	1132	..	12 5	1240	..	1 27	2 32	..	4 37	4 52	..	6 17	7 10	..	8 0	9 45	1045
3½	Bodmin A	arr	8 8	9 5	..	9 23	1018	1140	..	1213	1249	..	1 35	2 40	..	4 45	5 0	..	6 25	7 18	..	8 8	9 53	1053
		dep	8 13	..	..	..	1038	..	..	..	1254	..	..	2 55	..	4 50	5 18	.	6 30	7 43	..	8S20	..	..
11	Wadebridge	arr	8 30	..	..	..	1058	..	..	..	1 11	..	..	3 12	..	5 7	5 36	..	6 47	8 0	..	8S40	..	..

Miles			Week Days only																				
			a.m	a.m	a.m	a.m	a.m	a.m	a.m	a.m	a.m	non		p.m	p.m	p.m		p.m	p.m	p.m		p.m	p.m	p.m
			E	S		F	S	E	K	S				S									S	
—	Wadebridge	dep	..	..	..	8 30	..	..	9 22	..	..	12 0	..	..	1 30	3 30	.	..	5 56	7 5	..	8 42	9 10	..
7½	Bodmin A	arr	..	..	..	8 55	..	..	9 43	..	..	1220	..	..	1 50	3 53	..	..	6 16	7 25	..	9 2	9 30	..
		dep	7 30	7 40	8 30	..	9 0	9 20	9 47	1115	1148	1225	..	1 10	1 55	4 0	.	6 0	6 43	7 30	..	9 18	..	1030
11	Bodmin Road	arr	7 37	7 47	8 37	..	9 7	9 27	9 55	1122	1155	1232	..	1 17	2 2	4 7	..	6 7	6 50	7 37	..	9 25	..	1037

A 1 mile to Southern Region Station **D** Through Train to Padstow (arr. 8 45 a.m.) **E** Except Saturdays

F Through Train from Padstow (dep. 8 10 a.m.) Calls at **Grogley Halt** 8 40 a.m. and **Nanstallon Halt** 8 44 a.m.

K Through Train from Padstow (dep. 9 10 a.m.) **S** or S Saturdays only

BR, Summer 1948

TABLE A - OFF PEAK AND SATURDAYS/SUNDAYS This service is Diesel hauled on Saturdays

	A					
BODMIN GENERAL dep	10.30	11.20	12.25	2.05	3.10	A - DIESEL TRAIN RUNS MONDAYS TO FRIDAYS ONLY MAY 25-JULY 3
Colesloggett Halt dep	10.38	----	12.35	----	3.20	
BODMIN PARKWAY arr	10.43	----	12.42	----	3.27	
BOSCARNE JCN arr	----	11.35	----	2.20	----	
	A					
BOSCARNE JCN dep	----	11.45	----	2.30	----	
BODMIN PARKWAY dep	10.45	----	12.53	----	3.38	
Colesloggett Halt dep	10.50	----	1.02	----	3.47	
BODMIN GENERAL arr	11.00	12.02	1.15	2.47	4.00	

FRIENDS OF THOMAS WEEKENDS

"Thomas the Tank Engine" and his friends will be visiting Bodmin 10-13 April & 7-10 Aug

BODMIN GENERAL dep	10.45	11.35	12.35	1.20	2.20	3.10	4.10
Colesloggett Halt dep	----	11.45	----	1.30	----	3.20	----
BODMIN PARKWAY arr	----	11.52	----	1.37	----	3.27	----
BOSCARNE JCN arr	10.58	----	12.48	----	2.33	----	4.23
BOSCARNE JCN dep	11.05	----	12.55	----	2.40	----	4.30
BODMIN PARKWAY dep	----	12.05	----	1.50	----	3.40	----
Colesloggett Halt dep	----	12.13	----	1.58	----	3.48	----
BODMIN GENERAL arr	11.20	12.25	1.10	2.10	2.55	4.00	4.45

This will be a steam and diesel operated service. © Britt Allcroft (Thomas) Ltd 1998.

TABLE B - PEAK Mondays to Fridays July 6 to September 4 except August 7 and 10 (See Friends of Thomas Weekends).

	D							B	B	C	C
BODMIN GENERAL dep	10.15	11.00	12.10	1.10	2.20	3.20	4.30	7.00	8.25	7.00	8.10
Colesloggett Halt dep	----	11.10	----	1.20	----	3.30	----	----	----	----	----
BODMIN PARKWAY arr	----	11.17	----	1.27	----	3.37	----	7.15	----	----	8.27
BOSCARNE JCN arr	10.25	----	12.25	----	2.35	----	4.45	----	8.40	7.20	----
	D							B	B	C	C
BOSCARNE JCN dep	10.30	----	12.35	----	2.45	----	4.55	----	8.50	7.30	----
BODMIN PARKWAY dep	----	11.28	----	1.38	----	3.48	----	7.25	----	----	8.38
Colesloggett Halt dep	----	11.37	----	1.47	----	3.57	----	7.52	----	----	8.57
BODMIN GENERAL arr	10.42	11.50	12.52	2.00	3.02	4.10	5.12	8.05	9.07	7.47	9.10

D - DIESEL TRAIN

B - PASTY/BISTRO SPECIAL - Runs Tuesdays Only July 21 to September 1

C - MURDER MYSTERY SPECIAL Runs Fridays Only July 24 to August 28

Bodmin & Wenford Railway, 1998

INDEX OF LOCATIONS